Expert Praise for Gregg Ward and *Restoring Respect* . . .

"If you're like me, you know the grief or elation of a conflict resolution process gone bad or gone well. As expertly outlined in *Restoring Respect*, Gregg Ward's Coaching for Respect™ process makes success much more likely. It will help you, help your employees, and your organization become more civil, respectful, and conflict-free."

Cynthia Burnham, SVP (retired)
UBS Financial Services Forum for
Alternate Issue Resolution (F.A.I.R.)

"Gregg Ward's new book *Restoring Respect* and the Coaching for Respect™ process he outlines in it are invaluable when you're committed to making a positive difference in your organization in teamwork, leadership, and culture.

Sally Helgesen, Premier Women's Leadership Expert
Bestselling Author, *How Women Rise*

"Master Corporate Executive Coach Gregg Ward locks into a leadership secret that we have forgotten . . . the 'might' of RESPECT. Gregg's book takes us through a tour de force process of how to bring it back into the workplace."

CB Bowman, CEO
Association of Corporate Executive Coaches
Author, *Courage to Leap & Lead*

"I strongly recommend *Restoring Respect* for anyone looking to advance their own understanding of how to reconcile work relationships when respect has been lost. It's easy to read and understand and provides you with the practical knowledge and tools needed to be an effective peacemaker."

Adam Noakes, Administrative Law Judge
Expert, Alternative Dispute Resolution

"Having worked with leaders for over 40 years as both a trainer and a coach, I know that what Gregg is providing in this book is foundational for any leader. Without mutual respect the leader's path is fraught with challenge and disappointment. With it, the leader's path becomes significantly easier. The wisdom in this book is worth learning and putting into practice."

Frank Wagner, Co-Founder Stakeholder Centered Coaching®
Thinkers50 Top 50 Leadership Coaches—2021
Author, *The Power of Total Commitment*

"In our current charged environment, Gregg Ward's new book, *Restoring Respect*, couldn't come at a better time. It's a powerful guide on how to lead with a positive attitude in a way that brings organizations together in every situation. It is a must read for every leader and their team!"

Maya Hu-Chan, Top 8 Global Solutions Thinker, Top Leadership Coach 2021
Bestselling author, *Saving Face: How to Preserve Dignity and Build Trust*

"Respect for each other is a critical component of any successful team and when lost can be extremely detrimental to morale and productivity. In his new book, Gregg Ward clearly and concisely outlines key steps that can be undertaken to restore respect if all parties are engaged. This approach has the potential to repair relationships and promote successful working environments."

Rachel Soloff, Ph.D.
Executive Director Research
Global Pharmaceutical Company

"As a leader in diversity, equity, and inclusion strategy and an experienced coach, I found this book and its hands-on framework to be exactly the guide we need right now. Ward's Coaching for Respect™ process is a powerful answer to the high-costs and contagious impact of lost respect and trust."

Sarah Chapman Bacerra, Founder/CEO
Trailblazing in Color

"If you are looking for a better way to regain respect in the workplace and to allow teams to function and even thrive, look no further than Gregg Ward's excellent book. *Restoring Respect* provides a step-by-step process for doing just that!"

Ana Melikian, Ph.D., Host of the Mindset Zone Podcast
Human Potential Expert

"As an executive coach who worked over two decades as a C-Level executive, I can say that *Restoring Respect* brings a much-needed process to restoring relationships in the workplace."

Jon Saunders, Executive Coach
Peak Leadership Academy

"This book is an authoritative and significant contribution to understanding a critical area of respect: Interpersonal Respect. All managers and leaders who are intent on bolstering respect in their organizations should read it."

Gerald L. Finch, Ph.D., Co-Director of The Respect Project—Latin America,
Professor of Management and Psychology
Universidad San Francisco de Quito

"As co-author of *The Respectful Leader* and a long-time colleague of Gregg Ward's, I know his outstanding work on leadership very well. What he's introducing in *Restoring Respect* is truly groundbreaking—that we don't have to give up on work relationships that have soured due to disrespect, and that it's entirely possible to bring people back together, restore respect and create outstanding business outcomes, even in the toughest situations."

Walter G. Meyer
Bestselling Author, *Rounding Third*

"Gregg Ward is a tremendous thought leader who, in his latest book, highlights a simple solution to the most complex relationship challenge any of us may face—the loss of respect. In this much-needed resource, Gregg provides actionable steps for restoring respect so we can get the most out of our work and lives."

Eddie Turner, Principal Consultant and Executive Coach
Linkage, Inc., Top 25 Thought Leader - Thinkers360

"When respect is missing it sucks the life out of teams and the professional relationships that we need to ensure success. If we all applied some of the simple steps outlined in *Restoring Respect*, we'd reduce stress and anxiety at work, increase candor and collaboration, and ultimately achieve better results together."

Morag Barrett, CEO of SkyeTeam
Author of *You, Me, We, and Cultivate: The Power of Winning Relationships*

"As a business executive as well as an executive coach working across the globe, I've learned that the meaning of the word 'respect' differs among people and cultures. Gregg, the great storyteller he is, has been able to weave his magic in a very human and entertaining way, allowing us to draw our own learning and conclusions on how a relationship crosses the bridge from being dysfunctional to becoming fully respectful."

Cellene Hoogenkamp
Founder & CEO, KokuaHub, On-Demand Coaching
Author, *The Key to World-Class Team Performance*

"In his latest book, Gregg Ward identifies key concepts around respect and provides a clear framework for resolving workplace conflict. As a former COO and now an executive coach specializing in working with abrasive executives, I applaud his focus on respect and restoring it whenever possible."

Jordan Goldrich MG100, MCEC, PCC
Founder/CEO, Workplace Warrior Inc.
Author, *Workplace Warrior: People Skills for The No-Bullshit Executive*

"In his work on Respectful Leadership™, Gregg Ward has created an incredible foundation of powerful leadership and coaching techniques. These contagious methods have led to cultural and behavioral changes that are the core standard for internal and external relationships. His latest book, *Restoring Respect*, expertly lays out a roadmap for managing disruptive and dysfunctional behaviors that have been ignored for far too long."

Joslyn Barroso
Director, Human Resources
Leonardo DRS—LE/EOIS/NIS

"I believe when we reflect on our careers and the colleagues, peers and bosses we have worked with, each one of us has experienced disrespect—whether it was overt or covert. Gregg Ward takes the reader on a practical and straightforward 10-step journey to recognizing, understanding and addressing this type of conflict to restore relationships and ultimately build a more inclusive and positive workplace. *Restoring Respect* is a must have for your business and professional development bookshelf!"

Allison Akers Davis
Leadership and Organization Development Expert
Master Corporate Executive Coach
Founder and President Akers Davis

Also by Gregg Ward

The Respectful Leader:
seven ways to influence without intimidation

Bad Behavior, People Problems, and Sticky Situations:
a toolbook for managers & team leaders

GREGG WARD

AUTHOR OF THE AWARD-WINNING,
BestSelling BUSINESS FABLE
THE RESPECTFUL LEADER

RESTORING RESPECT

A "how to" guide for supporting the repair
of broken work relationships

WINDING
CREEK PRESS

Cover & Interior Design & Layout: David Maxine

Requests to the Publisher for permission should be addressed in writing by mail to the Permissions Department
Winding Creek Press/The Center for Respectful Leadership
6161 El Cajon Blvd
Suite B282
San Diego CA 92115

Library of Congress Cataloging-in-Publication Data:
Library of Congress Cataloging-in-Publication Data has been applied for and is on file with the Library of Congress.

ISBN 978-1-931957-20-5 (paperback)
ISBN 978-1-931957-21-2 (PDF)
Printed in the United States of America
10 9 8 7 6 5 4 3 2 1

WINDING
CREEK PRESS

Dedicated to those who are committed to making a positive difference in the world through respect.

Table of Contents ◼

Foreword ◻

By Marshall Goldsmith

Respect is a fundamental element of a positive company culture, and yet, too often we find employees and managers behaving in ways that their colleagues perceive as disrespectful. The negative impacts of disrespect can be felt throughout a company—from breakdowns in team communication, frustration with work or the organization, a decrease in motivation and collaboration, to shutting down or checking out completely.

As an Executive Coach for over 40 years, I am passionate about helping successful people get even better. I learned early in my career that executive coaching not only helps leaders in their professional lives, but also positively impacts their personal relationships and family life as well. When we learn to change behaviors that are detrimental to the trust, respect, and efficiency of our teams and company, we learn better communication skills that translate into success in profound ways.

In Gregg Ward's latest book, *Restoring Respect: a how-to guide for supporting the repair of broken work relationships*, he takes coaching to the next level. Gregg's created a unique, ten-step process called *Coaching for Respect*™, which is designed to support leaders and coworkers in addressing conflicts due to disrespect issues. This book provides a clear understanding of how respect functions in relationships, the disconnects that can come up, and a powerful process that restores respect and gets folks back to working well together again.

Ward, the Founder and Executive Director of the Center for Respectful Leadership, is an expert on this topic and has been helping leaders and teams recover from toxic, disrespectful work relationships and cultures for decades.

Restoring Respect

Restoring Respect covers key concepts on respect and disrespect and introduces some very useful neuroscience to help readers better understand root issues. It then outlines the essential techniques of coaching and facilitation before diving into the ten-steps of the *Coaching for Respect*™ (*CfR*) process Gregg has developed.

An excellent, no-nonsense writer, Gregg lays out the process well, provides specific goals for each step, and even recommends the language you should use to effectively run it.

Also, Gregg makes it clear you don't have to be an expert coach to run the *CfR* process. You could be in HR, learning and development, legal, a board member, or even a retired senior manager who has the people skills and genuine desire to help people work better together. All you'll need are good listening skills, a bit of patience and emotional intelligence, and the persistence to follow the process step-by-step while keeping yourself calm, focused, purposeful, and of course, respectful.

As I see it, any well-thought-out book and process that helps us create more respectful work environments is a real winner. *Restoring Respect* is exactly that.

—Marshall Goldsmith
Thinkers50 #1 Executive Coach
New York Times Bestselling Author of
The Earned Life, Triggers, and
What Got You Here Won't Get You There

Respect is like air. As long as it's present, nobody thinks about it.
But if you take it away, it's all that people can think about.
—from the book, Crucial Conversations.

Section I ◼
Before You Dive In

Is This What You're Looking For?

If you're in one of these roles . . .

✓ Human Resources, Leadership Development
✓ Executive Coach, Employee Relations, Organization Consultant
✓ In-House Attorney, Dispute Resolution Expert, Mediator, Ombudsperson
✓ Senior Executive, Emeritus Advisor, Board Member
✓ Frustrated Manager, Employee

. . . and you've seen what I'm about to describe, and you've been thinking, "There has to be a better way," then this book is for you.

Same Old, Same Old. Usually, when coworkers and/or managers and their subordinates lose respect for one another and their relationship dynamic starts to impact their work and the work of the people around them, the typical organizational responses include well-meaning exhortations to "just get along," generalized private chats with the participants by Human Resources, senior management, or supportive colleagues, or, quite often, no action at all.

If someone's disrespectful behavior is determined to have approached or crossed a policy or legal line, then an investigation may be launched, followed by disciplinary action, or interventional coaching, a lateral transfer, demotion, or termination. Even retaliation and/or constructive discharge may occur, or— once again—no action at all.

Restoring Respect

Even with the best of intentions, typical outcomes from these organizational responses include people saying, "That's just how they are," continuing disrespect, decreasing performance, collaboration, teamwork, and productivity, increased distancing, resentment, tension, disengagement, hostility, as well as potential for sabotage, plus turnover, resulting in loss of experience, intellectual capital, and productivity. Most people will agree that these are not particularly desirable outcomes.

Based on my work over more than two decades, it's obvious that most organizations would prefer to see more positive outcomes, but don't necessarily know how to get there.

A Better Outcome. Ideally, most organizations want to see a relationship in which respect has been lost return to a level of functionality to the point where the participants can work well enough together to meet organizational goals and key performance indicators (KPI's) over a sustained period without further significant issues or negative impacts to the organization.

This book, and the *Coaching for Respect*™ (*CfR*) process it outlines, is designed to help you and your organization achieve these goals.

Backstory to the process. I developed the *CfR* process in the early 2010's, after extensive coaching, facilitation, and mediation training, exposure to alternative dispute resolution techniques, and obtaining credentials and experience serving as an executive coach to hundreds of leaders in global businesses and government, many of whom wanted me to help them address what they call "personality conflicts" in their organizations.

At that same time, because of my knowledge of and passion for respect and Respectful Leadership™, I concluded that since I can coach co-workers who'd lost respect for each other back to the point where they have enough mutual respect to work again together reasonably well, then it might be useful to others if I were to outline my step-by-step process so that they could do the same. That process is what this book is all about.

I should say however, that if I'd only been trained as a coach without exposure to mediation or alternative dispute resolution concepts, or if I'd only been trained as a facilitator in conflict resolution or as a mediator without serving as a coach, I doubt I would have been able to develop the *CfR* process. My experience as a middle child, a Little League umpire, and as a husband and parent also helped.

Is This What You're Looking For?

But perhaps one of greatest influencing experiences I've ever had—in relation to developing the *CfR* process—occurred long before I became any of those things.

Back in the 1980's, when I was a young, starving professional theater artist in New York City, I fell into a job working for the New York City Police Department. I was tasked with working with a team of experts on developing a training program that used the techniques of professional theater and improvisation to teach officers to successfully manage what the police call "Emotionally Disturbed Persons" (EDP's). For over two years, I worked directly with world class police psychologists, hostage negotiators, members of the Emergency Services Unit, veteran beat cops, and distinguished professors at John Jay College of Criminal Justice to create a groundbreaking training program that would prove to be far more successful than anyone had anticipated.

I learned that it is possible, if you are careful, compassionate, respectful, and purposeful, to support people effectively through an emotionally loaded crisis brought on by feeling disrespected by others, or by an accusation of disrespect toward others. I learned you can guide them on de-escalating themselves, gaining new perspectives, and in choosing positive and productive paths forward. The *CfR* process is essentially a distillation of that formative experience, plus everything I learned, experienced, and practiced subsequently.

What is *CfR*? *Coaching for Respect*™ is a ten-step process that uses concepts around respect and disrespect, along with relationship coaching, psychology, and conflict and alternative dispute resolution techniques to facilitate and support the restoration of some level of respect to, and the repair of, work relationships that have become dysfunctional due to loss of respect.

So, if you have colleagues who have fallen out with each other due to perceived disrespectful behaviors, and *if* you have the willingness, the positional authority, the coaching and conflict resolution skills, and the patience to try something supportive and collaborative first, and *if* the participants are genuinely willing for you to try this strategy with them, and *if* legal and HR have signed off (I know, that's a lot of "*ifs*"), then the *CfR* process may be exactly what's needed to help turn that relationship around.

> In summary, this book is for you if you're looking for a process to help you support colleagues who genuinely want to rebuild their work relationship after respect between them has been lost.

Restoring Respect

At the Center for Respectful Leadership, which I founded in 2019 because of my own personal mission and passion around this topic, we believe the *CfR* process is a viable option when people lose respect for each other. It's something every organization should *consider trying first* (even if they rule it out), before moving on to more formal, investigative, disciplinary, and legal remedies.

At the core of this process is a simple question: *what do you respect in the other person?* We've found that when co-workers fall out over disrespectful behavior or language, what they do respect in their colleagues isn't completely obscured. It's just being overridden by strong negative feelings. Once the "what happened," the intentions, the impacts and perceptions have been uncovered and explored through coaching and rational discussion, the attributes that they do respect in one another become easier to see. Then, after genuine apologies have been made, the process builds on these respected attributes to create a "behavioral bridge" to a functional relationship going forward.

But we also want to make it clear that *CfR* is a voluntary process; participants must willingly choose to engage in it. No one should be forced, coerced, or mandated to participate, or threatened if they don't, because if they are, it will fail and possibly make things worse for everyone.

What Does It Take? It's important that you know that facilitating this process isn't a walk in the park; and it's not something anyone can do. *CfR* takes time, and you'll need to have some facilitation and coaching experience and acumen. It also takes emotional intelligence, patience, the willingness and authority to shut the process down, and the self-management skills to stay present, calm, and focused while the people you're coaching are in denial or emotional, resistant, manipulative, or downright ornery.

This is one of the many reasons why we have established a *CfR* Certification program at the Center for Respectful Leadership and strongly encourage you to take it. It's designed to provide you with a solid grounding in the concepts and the process, and some "real world" practice using it in experiential learning sessions with live, professional actors improvising in what we call "living case studies," so that you'll be fully prepared to run it when the need occurs.

Not Guaranteed, Sorry. It's also important to know that the *CfR* process is not guaranteed to work every time. There are simply too many variables, including people lacking in self-awareness, or being insincere or out of integrity,

Is This What You're Looking For?

competing personal agendas, organizational politics, and the possibility that one or both the participants considers the other's behavior to be what we call an "unrightable wrong" (more on this later). Often as not, these variables will stall or derail the process completely.

But many agree that *CfR* is worth trying, especially since both participants will benefit from having gone through it (even if the relationship isn't repaired), making future problems less likely.

Bottom line, if the participants have a genuine desire to repair their relationship and are willing to look at and "own" their own disrespectful behavior while charting a new course for change and committing to it, then the chances of a decent outcome via the *CfR* process are good. And, if it does work, then a heck of a lot of angst, time, effort, and money will be saved, which is a win-win for any organization and for the people directly involved.

A Work In Progress. As the creator of the *CfR* process, I should add that it's always a work in progress. I learn something new about how to do it "better" every time I run it. And I'll admit that I occasionally skip a step or spend a lot more time on another simply because my gut and experience tell me I should. These are two more compelling reasons why becoming certified in *CfR* is a good idea.

Thank You! Lastly, we thank you for your interest in *CfR*, your willingness to consider using it, and your openness to the possibility that respect can be restored within broken work relationships if there's a genuine desire by all to do so. Please let us know how we can help and support you.

Respectfully Yours,

—**Gregg Ward** MCEC, BCC
Founder | Executive Director
Center for Respectful Leadership
Hello@RespectfulLeadership.org

A Reason Not To. A word of caution: as you read through this book and learn about the process, and you come to feel that *CfR* is not something you're comfortable facilitating, then I urge you to trust your instincts. It's better that you choose not to facilitate the process if you're anxious about doing so, or if you feel that as an insider, you're unable to remain objective, or if the organizational politics are working against you or the goals of the process.

Restoring Respect

Instead, reach out to us and we'll identify *CfR*-Certified external coaches who may be able to help. Often, bringing in an impartial outsider to run the process is much more effective and can have a greater chance of success.

I would try to make sure that I and my friends were always treated with respect. Whether anyone likes me or not is irrelevant. The relevant thing to me was to be respected, and by being respected myself and by being respectful, it could create an atmosphere where the folks around me were also to be respected.
—Bill Russell

Section II ▣
Respect Matters

Before using the *CfR* process, you should have a solid understanding of what respect and disrespect are, the neuroscience involved, the impact they have on work relationships, and how they function depending on culture, personal experience, unconscious biases, personality, and communication style.

This section is a primer on respect and disrespect and is designed to support you with important information and concepts as you prepare to run the process. (NOTE: For a deeper dive and different learning experience, you might also want to engage with our suite of self-directed, e-Learning programs on respect that we call *The Roadmap2Respect* which you can access via the Center for Respectful Leadership's website.)

What Is Respect? We've found that most people don't think about respect very much unless there's a lack of it. And then, that's all they think about. Turns out that respect in work relationships is far more important than most of us think it is.

We'll start simply. At the Center for Respectful Leadership, we define respect as . . .

> **. . . feeling and displaying genuine admiration and appreciation for someone based on their abilities, qualities, achievements, and/or position, or simply because they're another human being.**

Restoring Respect

To be clear, this definition focuses on one type of respect, what we call "interpersonal respect." (We've found that there are at least two or three other types of respect). Also, this is considered a "western" definition by most experts, since there are some cultures that have varying historic and societal expectations around what is considered respectful behavior—such as, bowing as part of a greeting, making direct eye contact, or avoiding it, and who is automatically deserving of respect—such as your elders and those in authority.

Historically speaking, throughout most of the modern industrial era, if workers talked about interpersonal respect at all, then they expressed the idea that feeling respected at work was a nice-to-have, rather than a key motivator. Many workers—especially those at the lowest levels—had few expectations of being respected, believing instead that workers weren't "deserving" of their bosses' respect unless they'd "earned it." As for bosses, many assumed that they would be automatically respected by their workers for no other reason than their job title. They assumed that workers should know this and behave accordingly.

Sadly, old perceptions and traditions die hard. Today, in many organizations and cultures, these traditional "rules of interpersonal respect" are still very much in play. But the fact is, we're in a much different work world now, and just about everything has changed.

Today, due to advancements in psychology, research in neuroscience, on-the-ground experience by experts, the massive changes wrought by technology, the pandemic, and generational expectations, we now have a much greater understanding of the nature of respect. And we can see its impact on work relationships, productivity, engagement, and collaboration in ways we never have before.

We've learned that feeling respected matters much more to employees than once believed. Research shows that if your employees feel respected, valued, trusted, and treated kindly, then they are much more likely to stay with your organization. They will be more likely to treat your customers with respect, put in the extra hours and effort when the going gets tough, and remain upbeat and resilient in the face of challenges. As a bonus, they'll usually be happier.

Sadly, according to several recent, reputable, large-scale studies, and extensive research, it appears that disrespect and incivility are much more common and have greater negative impacts than previously thought. This is strongly supported by expert analysis of tens of thousands of reports of disrespect posted on anonymous, online rater sites like Glassdoor and Comparably, workplace cultural surveys that have been made public, and industry assessments.

Respect Matters

Before we go any further, it's important that we make a distinction between disrespect in the workplace and other, even more destructive, unlawful types of behavior including theft, fraud, industrial sabotage, vandalism, violence, violent bullying, threats of physical harm, and sexual harassment. These all, in one way or another, cross over a particular line into what many experts call "deviant workplace behavior." The *CfR* process is not a viable option with deviant workplace behaviors.

Secondarily, there is a broader category of behaviors that many experts are calling a "toxic work environment," which we at the Center for Respectful Leadership define as . . .

". . . a culture where employees feel disrespected on a regular basis, where diversity, equity and inclusion are not valued, and where unethical practices are tolerated or even encouraged."

If an organization is being repeatedly labeled by more than just a handful of employees as a "toxic work environment," then, again, the *CfR* process is not a viable option.

And there is one other area in which *CfR* is not a viable option: with people who have some type of psychiatric or personality disorder including sociopathy, narcissism, avoidant and antisocial personality disorders, among others. If you have concerns about someone's behavior that might make you suspect these disorders, we strongly recommend you consult with a qualified medical professional before considering *CfR*.

The *CfR* process is designed specifically to be used to help restore respect to a relationship in which the behaviors listed below have occurred once or twice (or perhaps a few times more) and the participants involved would still like to continue to work together and are genuinely looking for help. Or leadership and/or HR believes that the work relationship may be recoverable and are looking for a way to make that happen. Those behaviors include, but are not limited to . . .

- Foul language directed at others
- Derogatory name calling / demeaning / belittling / negative labeling
- Interrupting / ignoring others during meetings and conversations
- So-called "jokes" at others' expense
- Stereotyping, negative, and insulting remarks relating to, for example, co-workers' appearance, clothing, body type, weight, ethnicity, gender,

gender identity, sexual orientation, race, marital status, parental status, pregnancy, age, intelligence, experience, education, class, region, country, religion, politics, etc.

- Yelling / intimidation / sarcasm / bullying
- Throwing / smashing things at work
- Having a "this is me, so get used to it / get over it" attitude
- Incommunicative / withholding / lying
- Micro-managing / hovering / being constantly critical and negative
- Blaming and shaming / throwing under the bus
- Laziness / taking credit for someone else's work
- Distracted by phones and computers during meetings
- Malicious gossiping
- Enabling, allowing / failing to intervene when others are disrespectful

Sadly, this is not an exhaustive list, but these are the behaviors that are most frequently mentioned when we poll clients and training program participants about disrespectful behaviors they've experienced at work.

The challenge here is that many may consider these behaviors to be of no great consequence, believing that people need to toughen up and "grow a thicker skin," that this is just what happens in every workplace, and that people should just keep their heads down and do their jobs. They may also contend (correctly) that most people aren't sociopaths and narcissists intentionally disrespecting their co-workers to manipulate, denigrate and otherwise create upset and mayhem. They're convinced that in general, most of us are good people who don't intend to offend others and therefore should be given a pass on the stuff we say provided it doesn't cross the line into unethical, deviant, and illegal behavior.

At the Center for Respectful Leadership, we respectfully disagree with this "give-'em-a-pass" attitude, and point to considerable research that makes it abundantly clear that disrespectful behaviors—regardless of intent—are very problematic and can have measurably negative impacts on morale, turnover, performance, productivity, and collaboration. We're convinced that any leader who engages in, ignores, minimalizes, or tolerates disrespectful behavior is making a grave business, and potentially career-derailing, mistake.

Here's some data that proves our point. According to Harvard Business Review, researchers at Georgetown University and Arizona State University conducted multiple, large scale employee surveys and noted some troubling findings which we've summarized here:

Respect Matters

In response to being treated with incivility and disrespect, more than three-quarters of survey respondents indicated that they lost time at work thinking about the incident(s) and that their commitment to their employer had lessened. Two-thirds indicated that their performance had declined as well.

Bottom line, if you've got employees feeling disrespected by each other, their managers, or your customers or vendors, then it's going to negatively impact your business in some way. That's a fact. It's time the world's business leaders accepted this reality and stopped trying to shrug it off as just a bunch of snowflakes whining or politically correct sensitivity. Just because the boss doesn't value respect, doesn't mean it isn't important.

Additionally, several related studies indicate that women are more likely to perceive, experience, and report disrespect and incivility at work than men, although why they are more attuned to it, who is engaging in disrespectful behavior more (men or women), and the reasons why they're doing so are still being researched. Some researchers find that groups of men working together are less likely to notice or report disrespect and are more likely to engage in it as a kind of group or team bonding behavior. While this may not be a major problem for all-male teams, given today's increasingly diverse workforce, it's safe to say that disrespect should not be minimalized. Besides, if disrespect is the accepted norm in one part of your organization, it's likely to infect other parts as well.

Perhaps most importantly, the research indicates that work cultures which are considered "toxic" have significantly worse business outcomes across the board, including missed deadlines, mistakes, poor quality, higher conflict requiring expensive investigations, absenteeism, "presenteeism," and turnover. Interestingly, experts believe that this has very likely always been the case, but very few have spent the time and effort to study, document, and broadcast this fact, nor has organizational leadership—except in a few instances—ever seemed to care about it, until now, when our work environments are more diverse than they've ever been.

Another recent major study[1] conducted by MIT's Sloan School of Business, identified a "toxic work environment," as the number one reason people left their jobs during the so-called "Great Resignation," which we at the Center for Respectful Leadership prefer to call "The Great Reconsideration."

---

1 Donald Sull, Charles Sull, and Ben Zweig, *Toxic Culture Is Driving the Great Resignation* (MIT/Sloan Management Review, January 11, 2022)

Restoring Respect

According to this study, a "toxic work environment" was ten times more likely to lead to someone quitting than poor or unequal compensation.

Additionally, research shows that today's workers "expect" (although they hesitate to use this word), to be respected at some level, either for their knowledge and experience, their talents and skills, and the way they treat others. Although this applies to everyone, this is especially true with so-called "millennial" and "Generation Z" workers.

When today's managers utilize what are now considered old-school leadership styles such as "command-and-control," and "carrot-and-stick," many employees will feel disrespected. Even more troubling, many managers who employ these styles either don't know their behavior is considered disrespectful by their employees (often because no one has had the courage to call them on it, or because their leadership condones or ignores it), or worse, they simply don't care.

To be fair, both these leadership styles are entirely appropriate in certain work environments, such as in the military where command-and-control leadership saves lives, and in business development, where carrot-and-stick is an effective motivator in terms of driving sales. But, in general, when lives aren't at stake, and people aren't selling on commission, these two leadership styles are no longer nearly as effective, nor as tolerated by employees as they once were.

This means, if you're running the *CfR* process with a manager and their direct report, there's a strong likelihood that you'll be doing so with an employee who feels disrespected in some way by their boss and a boss who is either unaware or uncaring about it, or vice versa.

To sum all this data up, most people want to feel genuinely respected at work and if they are, then work outcomes will be better.

As a bonus, that feeling of respect is likely to be transferred to colleagues, customers, vendors, and the community.

Respectful workplaces are happier, more productive, and resilient. But if employees feel disrespected, then they, and the organization, will experience significantly negative business outcomes that are too costly to be ignored.

Respect Matters

The Neuroscience of Respect. Recent findings in neuroscience by Drs. Joseph LeDoux, Christine Porath, and many other experts on emotions and workplace relationships have confirmed what many of us sensed at a gut level: that feelings of respect and disrespect are just that, "feelings," and not the immediate result of cognitive, rational thought. In fact, we're now coming to understand that feeling respected or disrespected is the result of activities that occur deep within the most primitive parts of your brain.

Here's how it works. And please forgive the oversimplification of one of the most complex physiological processes found in the human body.

First, it's important to remember that our brains are "hard wired" to protect us from external threats, including those that are psychological as well as physical.

Here's how most of us respond to threats:

- In general, threats are first identified in the brain stem, a dense bundle of nerves at the base of the brain that acts as a kind of central processor that is continuously aggregating and analyzing all the neural inputs and stimuli that our senses (including your emotional sensors, or what some call "sixth" or "subliminal" senses) pick up.

- When someone treats you in a way that *you feel* is disrespectful (note: the phrase "in a way that *you feel* is disrespectful" is important because not everyone feels disrespected by the same behaviors), your brain stem's primitive threat sensors are triggered. Within milliseconds, this information flows to a part of the brain known as the amygdala, which (again, forgive the oversimplification) acts as a kind of "drug store" for the body, issuing prescriptions to the glands for the release and distribution and regulation of hormones coursing through your body at any given time.

- Essentially, when you're "feeling" disrespected, it means your body is quickly filling up with very powerful hormones, including adrenaline, cortisol (the "stress" hormone), and norepinephrine (a kind of neural lubricant), which lead to increases in your heart and breathing rates, your muscles tensing for action, and a general physical preparation to go into what is known as "fight, flight, or freeze" mode, also known as an "amygdala hijack." This activity occurs very rapidly, within a matter of seconds.

Restoring Respect

- At this point, your body's natural protective systems have taken over. This is instinctive, and because your brain and body have been hijacked to support your flight, fight, or freeze modes, there isn't a whole lot of rational, higher-level, cognitive thinking going on anymore.

- This means that if your natural tendency is to react to disrespect by fighting back, you may be unable to control yourself and you may say or do something disrespectful in return. If your tendency is toward flight when feeling disrespected, you might quickly leave the situation (if you can). And, if you tend to freeze when feeling disrespected, you may say or do nothing and shut down. But, in all cases you'll still have a physical reaction, and—for a while—a hard time thinking clearly or focusing on anything other than the disrespectful thing that was done or said to or about you.

- Adding to the problem, once the initial threat of feeling disrespected has passed, it can take many minutes, and sometimes an hour or more for your body to settle down to its previous calmer state. Note that you can't consciously "will" yourself to calm down. The best you can do when you're in the middle of an amygdala hijack is to recognize it and breathe deeply and intentionally, attempting to slow your heart and breathing rates while relaxing your muscles. Taking a break from the situation can also help.

- If the disrespectful behavior is repeated by that same person, most people will unconsciously don a metaphorical pair of sunglasses with the words "disrespectful person" written on the lenses and will view the person who disrespected them through these glasses going forward. This is called "confirmation bias" (more on this soon).

- Finally, because of the way the brain sorts and stores memories, disrespect "sticks." People tend to remember unresolved disrespectful incidents as if they happened recently. They can often remember, in astonishing detail, events that happened months—or years!—prior.

However, if someone treats you in a way that you consider to be genuinely respectful, your primitive threat center is bypassed and your pituitary gland will release a hormone called oxytocin (also known as, the "bonding," or "love" hormone), into your body causing you to feel "good." Typically, as a result, you will reciprocate with respect toward them, causing their bodies to release oxytocin as well. As we like to say, respect is contagious. Unfortunately, so is disrespect.

Still, when it comes to disrespect, it's important to know that most of us will react in some way to feeling disrespected, despite our proclamations of being "tough," and having a "thick skin." In truth, although we may deny it, each of us has unique and specific triggers that will set off an amygdala hijack and seemingly irrational responses.

Of course, there are those who appear to be able to let disrespect roll off their backs. These folks tend to fall into three categories: First, people who have a great deal of self-confidence, emotional intelligence, self-control, and experience in dealing with disrespect. Second, people who are very positionally safe and secure and, third, people who have been repeatedly disrespected over a long period of time (such as police officers) and have become inured to it. But even then, most of us have an invisible line in the sand that, if crossed, will generate a threat reaction of some degree. In my experience working with police officers, this often occurs when someone—especially someone whom they believe has committed a violent crime—refuses to comply with their commands.

I'll admit, what I've just provided is a very simple and brief explanation of the Neuroscience of Respect and disrespect. There is much more to know. But we recommend you become reasonably familiar with the general concepts I've outlined, because when you're coaching people who are feeling disrespected, their understanding of this neuroscience may help them to put what we call the "what happened" (the facts around the language and behaviors that led to feelings of disrespect) into a more neutral perspective, which will allow them to move forward more easily.

Gunnysacking. Decades ago, when we first started looking at how respect and disrespect operate in work environments, our HR clients talked to us about something that we eventually started to call, "gunnysacking." As someone who is going to run the *CfR* process, you need to know about it, because it's very likely it will play a role.

For various reasons, including not wanting to be perceived as a complainer, worries about not being considered a team player, and/or fear of retaliation, most employees do not file a complaint with HR the first time they feel disrespected by a boss or colleague. Instead, they start carrying a metaphoric gunnysack over their shoulder, and quietly deposit incidents of disrespectful behavior into it while trying to suppress their feelings of anger, disbelief, frustration, surprise, hurt, and humiliation.

If an employee has been gunnysacking and burying their feelings for a while, then it's possible that one day someone will disrespect them—sometimes in ways that others consider to be inconsequential—and they will unexpectedly snap, and vent their pent up anger and frustration, sometimes destructively.

Somewhat more often, after their invisible gunnysack has become too heavy to ignore, they decide it's time to go to HR and file a formal complaint by dumping the contents of the sack out on the desk of the poor HR person, who then almost always wonders (sometimes out loud), "Why am I only hearing about this now?"

But, these days, the most common result of gunnysacking is that the employee who feels disrespected says nothing to HR, starts looking for another job, and once they find one, they quit, and may decide to unload their gunnysack during the exit interview (if there is one). If they are lucky enough to hear it, the HR person is left thinking that they might have been able to prevent the loss of a good employee, and related costs, if they'd only known sooner about what had been going on and had a chance to do something about it—like running the *CfR* process!

You need to be aware of gunnysacking and how it impacts work relationships. This is because, at the start of the *CfR* process, you'll be having private, separate one-on-one meetings with each of the participants during which they'll describe the "what happened," i.e., the incident(s) that occurred, and all of the disrespectful behavior or language that they perceived was targeted at or about them that caused them to feel disrespected. They're going to unload their gunnysack in front of you, which is fine, because you need to see what's in it, and they need to be and feel "heard."

Typically, as they unload, they'll use emotionally descriptive words and phrases about the incidents, their feelings, and the people who disrespected them like "humiliated," "betrayed," "shocked," "embarrassed," "stunned," "hurt," "childish," "jerk," "surprised," "disgusting," "disrespected," and/or "confused." These are very common reactions to disrespect and if you think back to a time when you felt disrespected, it's likely that you would also use one or more of these words to describe your feelings about the incidents and the people who disrespected you.

Respect Matters

While someone is unloading their gunnysack in front of you, you may also notice that they're becoming upset and agitated, even though the person who disrespected them isn't around. This is because, as they tell their story using the language of emotions, they are re-experiencing how they felt at the time. You might notice physical changes in them, such as elevated breathing or tension, and they might report an increasing heartbeat or sickly feeling in their gut. They may become angry, depressed, or teary. All of this is normal and to be expected.

As the coach, it's valuable for you to know that when people specifically name the feelings they experienced during an incidence of disrespect, and then continue to do so during subsequent coaching sessions, they'll eventually be better able to discuss the incident more objectively, with less emotional re-triggering and coloring. In standard psychological practice, listening to someone recount the "what happened," and then discussing their feelings about it and the people involved, is known as "talk therapy."

As the coach of the *CfR* process, knowing about talk therapy is useful because eventually, toward the end, you'll be asking each person to examine their own behavior and/or language dispassionately and describe the "what happened" (as they experienced it) to the other participant as factually as possible during the joint coaching session. So, you can imagine that if they're still fully re-experiencing negative emotions when they're describing the incident to the person who disrespected them, it will be that much harder for you to make progress toward helping them repair the relationship. This is one of the many reasons you will *not* be bringing the two participants together at the beginning of the *CfR* process. They're simply not ready.

In the early sessions, it's imperative that you allow and encourage the participants to talk with you privately about their feelings, which are the result—as we've established—of the very deep-seated and primitive brain processes that are wired into us as human beings. You'd be well-advised to have a box of tissues handy when you conduct these initial sessions, not only for them, but for you too if you're a particularly empathetic person.

The Trust Gap. Many people believe that respect and trust go hand in hand. We agree. When someone engages in what we consider to be disrespectful behavior, and it is directed at us, not only do we have a physiological response, but when we start to think about the "what happened," we may begin to feel as if we don't trust that person as much as we did before. This means that the "Trust Gap" is increased between us and them. Closing that gap completely, or at least narrowing it, is part of restoring respect to any relationship. Sometimes, however, the behavior is so egregious that we feel we cannot trust that person anymore and that restoring respect to the relationship is not possible.

Confirmation Bias and "Unrightable Wrongs." Theres's one more important piece of neuroscience that you'll need to know about before you run the *CfR* process for the first time: it's an unconscious mechanism previously mentioned earlier called "confirmation bias," and it's closely related to gunnysacking.

In addition to being wired to sense and protect us against threats, the human brain also tends to look continuously for patterns of behavior and to categorize them in a simple binary fashion: threat/no threat, feels good/feels bad, and hurts me/doesn't hurt me. This is instinctive. Once we feel threatened by certain behaviors and/or language, we tend to want to protect ourselves from it happening again, so we'll be unconsciously (sometimes consciously) on the lookout for it.

If the same person engages in similar disrespectful behavior toward us again, we'll put on those metaphorical sunglasses we mentioned, and we might even experience a fight/fight/freeze reaction the next time we see them, even though they aren't behaving disrespectfully in that moment. It's like being beaten up by the schoolyard bully once, and then every time you see them again, even though they may be ignoring you, you can't help but feel anxious.

This means that confirmation bias plays a role in most interpersonal conflicts, and as the coach you need to look and listen for it when people are describing the "what happened" during your initial private one-on-one sessions. By then, they may have been gunnysacking that person's behavior for some time. During your initial *CfR* sessions, you'll need to be able to gauge the weight of their gunnysack and the permanence of their "disrespectful person" sunglasses. You need to be aware that some confirmation biases are so locked in and secure, that no amount of coaching will ever get them to see any aspects of the person who disrespected them in any other light than a negative one.

If this is the case, then you may be dealing with someone who considers the other person's behavior or language to be an "unrightable wrong," something that in their mind is so heinous and so over-the-line, that no amount of coaching or sincere apology or repeated attempts at amends will ever change their perception. As I mentioned earlier, you'll need to consider the possibility that the behavior under discussion is outside of what *CfR* is designed to help address.

Respect Matters

If you're coaching someone who is convinced, (remember, it's all about feelings, not rational thinking), that they were the target of an "unrightable wrong," you will need to work very hard to coach them past their confirmation bias, to the point where they will admit that they actually have that bias and that there may be other equally valid yet different perspectives on the "what happened" that they should consider in order to move forward. Rationally considering others' perspectives is a key component of the *CfR* process. But it isn't easy for the average person, not by a long shot. Heck, it's not even easy for experts!

Unfortunately, if you're unsuccessful coaching someone past their confirmation biases and their strongly held belief that they've been the target (I never say "victim," people don't like being labeled victims) of an unrightable wrong, then you may be dealing with someone who has decided that they simply can't work with the other person anymore. In that case, a restoration of respect and a return to a productive relationship is just not going to happen.

This means that like it or not, you'll have to shut the *CfR* process down. Believe me, several times over the years I've had to shut the process down during the initial stages due to confirmation biases and perceived unrightable wrongs. No matter how hard I tried, there was no moving them off their perception (often as not, because the other person had truly engaged in egregiously disrespectful behavior), and it became clear to all stakeholders that the process was just not going to be helpful.

You should know that at the Center for Respectful Leadership, we always inform our client's HR leadership in advance about the nature of "unrightable wrongs," and how they could completely derail the *CfR* process. You must do the same because all stakeholders need to be aware of the potential for unrightable wrongs to stop the *CfR* process in its tracks, permanently.

This is one of the main reasons you must never guarantee that you can "fix" a relationship using the *CfR* process.

Another challenge is that some people do feel "victimized" by what they perceive as disrespect and use this as an "excuse" for reduced productivity, or shutting down, or refusing to be held accountable. They may have trouble understanding that it is possible to develop the psychological muscle to separate their self-esteem from how others treat them; that they still can be confident and carry on despite being treated with disrespect.

For an example of someone who refused to let open and public disrespect define him or his actions, we should consider Mahatma Gandhi, who was arrested and imprisoned many times, not to mention the verbal and physical abuse he suffered over his long career in non-violent protest. Having the personal fortitude not to allow oneself to be victimized by disrespect, and to carry on with work while treating others with respect can be valuable skills for success in business and in life, to say nothing of personal peace and fulfillment. Now, this is not to say we should ignore or minimize disrespect. We shouldn't. But we should not allow it to paralyze us or cause us to behave disrespectfully toward others, either.

Performative Respect and Other Expectations. As I mentioned earlier while defining respect, there are many cultures that have different stated and unstated expectations around respect, such as "you must respect your elders," or "you must respect those in authority."

Research indicates that many people who were raised with, or subscribe to these expectations, can experience a kind of unconscious confusion in their minds if the person they are required to respect behaves disrespectfully. Think of it this way: we're told we must respect someone like our grandparent or a police officer. But imagine they behave disrespectfully toward us or others. First, we know we could never get away with doing this ourselves without punishment or consequences. Secondly, we're still supposed to respect these folks? It doesn't compute.

So, many of us will engage in "performative respect," that is, going through the motions and saying things that are considered respectful by society, but not honestly feeling it in our hearts. In fact, many people, in all sorts of cultures, can engage in performative respect with ease. For example, they'll say "yes, sir," or "yes, ma'am," or "I respect you," when their tone of voice and body language clearly reveals a lack of a respect to those who are paying attention.

This is the problem with performative respect: most of us can sense when others are doing it. In fact, many people consider performative respect to be a passive/aggressive insult instead. This can lead to a greater chance of conflict.

As you coach in the *CfR* process, it's imperative that you explore the ingrained (and potentially unconscious) respect expectations of the participants. For instance, are you facilitating the process with someone who believes their boss must be respected no matter what, but is now engaging in a surreptitious work slowdown and sabotage because they feel disrespected by that same boss? Or do you have a boss who feels they're owed respect simply because of their title and authority and who feels disrespected by employees who are only engaging in performative respect?

Respect Matters

Vice versa, do you have an employee who has no respect for those in authority and refuses to even display performative respect toward them and is, in fact, deliberately behaving in a disrespectful manner because they are perhaps protected in some way and know they can get away with it? Or they know they can use the formal grievance system to undermine leadership? These are all things you'll need to inquire into and do so in a way that doesn't generate defensiveness.

On Communication Styles. At the Center for Respectful Leadership, we're big fans of a popular personal and professional development tool called the DISC (or DiSC) Communication Styles Assessment Instrument. DISC helps us to identify our natural and adaptive communication styles. It's technically not a personality test like Myers-Briggs (MBTI), The Hogan, or The Birkman Method, it's an assessment of behaviors—how you choose to show up when you communicate. It's been extensively validated and in wide use since the 1970's as a professional and leadership development tool. Although the DISC is one of several so-called "Four Quadrant" Personality Assessments (MBTI being perhaps the most famous), which have recently fallen into disfavor among academics, professional psychologists, and clinical research scientists, we see the DISC as a useful guide to common communication behavioral styles and how to adapt them to communicate more effectively.

Since both deliberate and unintentional miscommunication are often the root causes of people feeling disrespected, we strongly urge you to familiarize yourself with, or become certified in using the DISC. It's one of the simplest (and least expensive) assessments available and can be especially helpful to you and the participants you're coaching when facilitating the *CfR* process.

It's also helpful to be familiar with the DISC since it can help you determine which communication styles the people you're coaching consider to be respectful and disrespectful. Knowing their communication style preferences will give you a leg up on helping them understand how they communicate and want to be treated.

Unintentional Disrespect. Nine times out of ten, when someone is accused of engaging in disrespectful language or behavior, they'll say, "That's not what I intended," or, "I didn't mean to offend them." I recommend you accept this as sincere. Most people don't deliberately set out to disrespect another unless they've been provoked or disrespected themselves. During the *CfR* process:

what we intend is irrelevant; it's the impact of our behavior that matters. If someone feels disrespected, they feel disrespected. If you believe you should get a pass because you didn't intend to be disrespectful, that doesn't mean everything's okay, and we should all just get back to work. People still feel disrespected, and that will make it that much harder to work together if it's not addressed.

The Platinum Rule. Although it's common practice by many managers, *The Golden Rule* ("*Do unto others as you would have them do unto you.*") isn't always the best way to interact with others. We need to bear in mind that not everyone wants to be done unto the same ways as we do.

This is where *The Platinum Rule* ("*Do unto others as they would have you do unto them*") can be helpful to you as a coach. Coined by Dr. Tony Allessandra in his book of the same name, *The Platinum Rule* encourages us to consider how others want to be treated, rather than assuming that they want to be treated like we do. It's about being empathetic toward others, acknowledging that people are different—not better or worse—just different, and then adapting our own styles to communicate more effectively, meet them "where they are," and achieve better outcomes.

In today's increasingly diverse workplaces, acknowledging, appreciating, valuing, and adapting to differences is a business imperative if you want to retain your best and brightest, and drive results. So, when you're facilitating the *CfR* process you'll need to both remember *The Platinum Rule* yourself, and coach the participants on it too. It could very well make the key difference in whether the process is successful, or not.

Kindness. Defined as being "generous, benevolent, caring, respectful, and compassionate," kindness is not a word we hear used very much in the workplace. It should be. Numerous studies indicate that when employees and their managers treat their co-workers and customers with kindness—such as giving them genuine compliments and recognition—the positive impact on business outcomes is clear, and stated core values are perceived as real and genuine rather than just performative window dressing. We cannot overemphasize the value of being kind to others.

And yet, too many people believe that being kind is a display of weakness, that they'll be taken advantage of if they are kind, or that only the tough can compete. These beliefs have been consistently proven to be false, and yet they persist. If you're a leader and you want to create a culture where people willingly perform at their best repeatedly, consider making kindness, decency, and respect part of your core values and walk your talk every single day. You will not regret it.

Coaching Managers Who Believe Respect Has to Be Earned. I once coached a senior manager who said, "Nobody ever respected me when I first started out. I had to earn my boss's respect. Why is it any different now?"

This is a fair question, especially when it comes from someone who believes that employees need to earn the respect of their boss, not the other way around. The short answer is *because everything has changed.*

The world of work has changed dramatically in the past two decades, and the pandemic accelerated that change. Demographically speaking, baby boomers are heading into retirement faster than any other group, and in 2025 millennials, and Generation Z will comprise more than half of the global workforce. In terms of academic degrees, millennials and Gen-Z's are the most educated generations, ever.

They also know recent history and their place in it. For example, they know that the days of so-called "cradle-to-grave employment"—where you joined a company right out of high school or college and worked your way up over 40 years and then retired with a gold watch and a pension—are long gone.

These days, companies are hiring highly trained and experienced specialists to do certain jobs. And, if things don't go as planned, or if they aren't needed anymore, they lay them off as quickly as they hire them.

Many of today's younger workers also saw what happened during the Great Recession (2007-2011) where tens of millions of people lost their jobs and their homes almost overnight. They came to adulthood with valid concerns about financial stability and independence, and they know that very few companies are going to be loyal to them anymore. So, they are less loyal in return, and they expect to work for as many as 10 to 15 different companies during their career.

No, our millennial and Gen-Z workers are not fools (trust me, I should know, I'm a father to three of them). They know the world of work has fundamentally changed, and that because of their training and expertise, they are now in the driver's seat when it comes to choosing what company to work for. They will not tolerate being disrespected at work for very long.

But sadly, there are still people in our workplaces—in every generation and at every level—who are convinced that those old work paradigms and leadership styles are working just fine. This means that conflicts and disrespect between these folks and their colleagues are bound to surface.

There's another reason why the traditional view that employees need to earn the respect of their bosses doesn't work: it often backfires. Our research indicates that managers who insist that employees earn their respect are less likely to be respected. They may be obeyed, they may be feared, but they will not be respected. This makes working together that much more difficult for both. It's also a huge waste of time. You'd be amazed at how much time is lost from people dwelling on and discussing their boss's disrespectful behaviors with co-workers. Whether that's right or wrong of them is immaterial, they still do it.

So, it's more likely than not that you'll find that this clash of perspectives around respect—"respect matters" vs. "no, not really"—is a key issue in many of the relationships that you'll be trying to repair using the *CfR* process. Often, the difference between the two will be easy to spot: the person who feels disrespected has strong feelings about the "what happened," while the other thinks they're over-reacting. Often, telling someone their overreacting only tends to trigger an even stronger negative reaction. We've found during coaching that participants who feel disrespected by their boss regularly express that they feel frustrated, belittled and disempowered. So, during the joint session toward the end of the *CfR* process, they feel it's important to express their frustrations by saying, "You don't get to disrespect me and then tell me how I'm supposed to react to it."

Three Key Understandings. Before you get very far down the road in facilitating the *CfR* process, there are three "key understandings" that the participants being coached must know about and agree are true and valid. I urge you to commit these to memory:

1. *"You don't have to like someone to work well with them, but you do have to have some level of respect for them."*
2. *"It-Takes-Two-To-Tango,"* and,
3. *"Who Can I Control? Only Me."*

You Don't Have to Like Someone to Work Well With Them, But. One of my first jobs was on a road cleanup crew where, as the newbie, I was given all of the "scut-work," like pulling broken appliances out of standing water, cleaning up food waste—you know, the stuff no one else wants to do. I understood that this was the way it was in this job. I had to pay my dues and generally suck it up and keep my head down.

However, there was one foreman, a guy not much older than me, who seemed to take a particular delight in making my life miserable. Right after I'd pulled an old stove out of a pond, he'd throw it back in and tell me to go get it. Or I'd finish filling a trash barrel and he'd tip it over and demand I clean it up. It was unbelievably disrespectful behavior and a waste of time by someone who was supposed to be a leader. I'll never forget what our supervisor said when I complained, "You don't have to like someone to work with them." Much as I didn't want to hear that, I realized he had a point.

Fortunately, many of us work with people we actually "like." In other words, we enjoy working with them, are pleased to be in their company, and we might even socialize with them outside of work. This is fine and healthy, and the work output and relationships are good. But it's also true that many of us work with people that we don't necessarily like, but from a performance perspective we're still working well together. This is because we have some level of respect for them.

Usually, we have respect for our colleagues in these areas:

- *Their knowledge and experience (and position attained as a result)*
- *Their talents and skills*
- *The way they treat us and others*

When you're running the *CfR* process, often you'll find that the participants don't like each other, or they did at one point, but not anymore. It's imperative that you help them understand the distinction between liking a co-worker and respecting them, because eventually, as you take them through the process, you're going to be coaching to help them identify what they do respect. They may not ever like each other again as they once did, but the process is designed to help them identify or re-identify what they respect in the other person. From there, the goal is to restore enough respect to the relationship so it can function effectively again.

It-Takes-Two-To-Tango. Most of us have heard the phrase, "It-Takes-Two-To-Tango," meaning people must deliberately work together to achieve a successful outcome. This holds especially true for the *CfR* process. If the participants being coached are not genuinely willing to commit to and honestly engage in what we call the "restorative dance" during and after the *CfR* process, then the chances of respect being restored, or staying in the relationship are low. As the coach, it's your job to ensure that they understand this concept at the beginning of the process and are continuing to dance genuinely with each other while going through it, and afterward.

It's also your job to notice when one or both are refusing to dance, which we call being "out of integrity." In other words, they appear to be deliberately making it difficult for the process to move forward. There are, of course, many reasons they might choose to mess up the dance or stop altogether, including the realization that their behavior was indeed disrespectful but they don't want to admit it, or feeling like the whole process is a bunch of psychobabble and a plot of some kind to undermine their agency or authority, or—as I've mentioned before—the belief that the other person has engaged in an unrightable wrong, making the restoration of respect the last thing they feel like doing.

In each of these cases, you're going to have to work hard to coach the individuals past their resistance. If you're unable to do this, then you're going to have to call it quits, and shut down the process permanently.

Who Can I Control? Only Me. In many relationships, one participant (or both) may attempt to control what the other does or says. Sometimes they're successful, but oftentimes they aren't, or at a minimum the controlled person feels disrespected, and possibly coerced or bullied. Very few of us will sincerely and willingly change our behavior under these conditions. It's like telling two kids who have just been fighting in the schoolyard to shake hands and make up with each other. They may shake hands under threat of suspension, but a genuine and sincere reconciliation isn't likely to happen in that moment, or maybe ever.

During your initial *CfR* meetings, you may find that one or both the participants may insist or have the expectation that if there's going to be a reconciliation and/or a restoration of respect, then the other person must change or do something, like apologize. It's your job to ensure that each participant understands that trying to force someone to change or apologize is likely to backfire and make things worse. Instead, the participants must understand that the only person they can control during this process is themselves. They must understand and authentically own this truth and chose what they're going to do and say to restore respect. If they don't, again, the process is likely to stall or be derailed and you'll have to shut it down.

Respect Matters

Of course, if someone wishes to genuinely apologize, then without question you should encourage and facilitate this. We've developed a model called a "Full Apology" which is introduced in Step Eight and comes into play during Step Nine. And we've found that a genuine apology during the joint session is one of the most important ways of restoring respect to any work relationship.

Given all of this, as I mentioned before and as you might imagine, facilitating the *CfR* process isn't easy. In fact, it may be one of the hardest things you will ever do. But if you're successful with it, it can be a very rewarding and satisfying experience for you and the people you're coaching.

Use the Glossary. I've covered many terms, concepts, and ideas in this part of the book and it's entirely possible I've overwhelmed you. For a quick reference, you'll find them listed alphabetically and summarized, along with many of the other terms I use in the Glossary at the back, starting on page 123.

Executives and HR managers know coaching is the most potent tool for inducing positive personal change, ensuring better than average odds of success and making the change stick for the long term.
—The Ivy Business Journal

Section III ◼
Coaching Matters

Before beginning to use the *CfR* process, you should have a reasonable understanding of what coaching—in the context of facilitating the *CfR* process—is, and what it's not.

What Is Coaching? As recently as the 1980's, when people referred to coaching, they were talking about sports—former athletes and other experts who would coach individuals or teams. That changed when coaching was first introduced to the business world in the UK by Sir John Whitworth and others who took concepts from sports coaching and refocused them into what they called "performance coaching" in the workplace.

Today, many types of coaching are available, including executive, strategic, life, career, performance, developmental, and team coaching, among others. The growth of coaching as a business success strategy has been rapid. In fact, in June of 2022, executive coaching in the US was estimated to be a $14B industry[1]. Top leaders all over the world credit the coaching they received along the way with helping them to achieve phenomenal success. There's no doubt that coaching has gone mainstream.

Sadly, many people react negatively to the word "coaching" because, in some organizations, it's been inappropriately used as a polite euphemism for putting someone on a PIP (Performance Improvement Plan), negative feedback, criticism, discipline, and corrective action. If you want to be effective using the *CfR* process, you'll have to find out peoples' perceptions of the word "coaching" and mitigate any negative and cynical attitudes they have about it early on.

Occasionally, people confuse coaching with mentoring, managing, or training. But they're very different. True coaching, in essence, involves respectfully challenging the person being coached to look directly at their individual, and/ or team, and/or business challenges, to establish goals, to identify what they want or need to change, and then supporting them in developing and executing a workable strategy for making those changes and achieving their goals. A manager who is truly coaching understands and follows this process, and makes it clear to the person that this is what they're doing.

Mentoring, on the other hand, typically involves a seasoned, senior leader with a lot of experience, connections, and knowledge—but not necessarily coaching training—who voluntarily chooses to advise and help position a more junior person with success in their career, organization, or industry. They'll often tell them who they should connect with, what hoops they need to jump through to be perceived as having leadership potential, how to solve problems, or when to bow out of a difficult situation. Occasionally, the mentor/mentee roles are reversed, and a younger, more junior employee will volunteer to serve as a mentor to a senior manager on how to effectively lead today's increasingly diverse employee populations.

Managing is also different than coaching, although it can be closer to mentoring. Like the sports coach, managing typically involves telling direct reports what to do, or at least setting goals for them and guiding and supporting them, and holding them accountable as they go after them. This is the primary work of most managers. It's invaluable, but it's not coaching.

As for training, I know many managers who think they're coaching when they're really training. Typically, when the manager observes their direct report and thinks that mistakes are being made or their performance could be improved, they'll say, "let me coach you," and then they'll tell them what to do or show them how to do it "better." Again, this isn't coaching other than in the athletic sense.

If a manager is truly coaching someone, they will start the conversation with a question: "Would you be open to some coaching?" Assuming the answer is "yes," they'll start to ask open-ended questions and make useful observations that provoke self-awareness, insights, and the desire and intention within the mind of the participant to solve their own problems and step up to challenges.

As a coach running the *CfR* process, you won't be managing or mentoring very much, although you might be doing a little training—such as training someone on how to make a Full Apology. But mostly, once you're past the initial steps, you'll be asking questions that cause the participants to think about themselves and their own behaviors and attitudes, how these impact others, and what they might want to change going forward.

True coaching is confidential, where the person being coached is comfortable sharing their thoughts and feelings with you, and you are employing a set of learned skills that include listening, asking thought-provoking questions, guiding discussions, brainstorming, providing encouragement, candid feedback, redirection, and de-escalating someone who's upset.

At the heart of coaching is a genuine desire by the coach to help and support others in learning how to help themselves so that they have greater self-awareness of how they may be "stuck" in old habits and mindsets, and guide them as they uncover new perspectives on the challenges they face, revise their goals, develop new ones, and identify pathways to self-improvement and success in meeting those goals.

Since coaching involves using many specific interpersonal and communication skills, many executive and leadership coaches—even those who'd previously headed up large corporations—choose to receive their coach training and credentials in intensive and rigorous programs where they are observed and critiqued by expert coaches in extensive practice sessions before being awarded their formal coaching certifications.

When it comes to facilitating the *CfR* process, while it's certainly helpful to have received training in a certified executive coach training program, it's not a "must have." I know many HR experts, retired executives, and leadership development professionals who have the right temperament and skill set, and enough experience and emotional intelligence to run the *CfR* process successfully once they've learned it, even though they're not extensively trained and credentialed executive coaches. And there are some highly trained coaches who cannot, for a variety of reasons, effectively facilitate the *CfR* process.

So, here's a list of the primary skills you'll need to effectively facilitate *CfR*:

- ✓ Patience, calmness, and ability to focus on seeing the process through.
- ✓ The ability to recognize your own biases and keep them from skewing

the process and to convince the participants that you're not taking sides.

- ✓ The listening skills that enable participants to be vulnerable and open up to you about their issues, feelings, and failings.
- ✓ To know how and when to ask the right kinds of questions that will provoke introspection, reconsideration, and behavioral change.
- ✓ The emotional intelligence, compassion, and sensitivity to move forward respectfully while effectively managing upset and/or resistance.
- ✓ Enough professional gravitas and so-called, "people skills" to ensure that when they come together, the participants behave respectfully while honoring their commitments to you and each other.

It's also very helpful to be able to sniff out insincerity, manipulation, out-of-integrity behavior, and political considerations on the fly.

What Coaching Isn't. Many managers and leaders are very good at fixing things, solving problems, and getting everyone aligned and headed in the same direction. These are valuable skills in terms of driving positive business outcomes. But, when it comes to coaching, employing these skills with people who've lost respect for each other can make the situation significantly worse.

A truly effective facilitator of the *CfR* process doesn't directly tell the participants what to do, what they should be thinking, or what changes they should be making. Instead, they're more like patient "guides" helping someone who has a willingness to engage in self-exploration, to examine their own behavior and how it impacts others, and to come up with their own goals and strategies for change.

Drawing from an ancient learning process called the "Socratic Method," the effective coach patiently keeps asking questions that generate introspection and reconsideration, which can eventually lead to "Ah ha! Moments," and even deeper revelations and insights about the "what happened" in their lives and relationships. This is especially important when you're running the *CfR* process, because having someone come to the realization themselves that they've been behaving disrespectfully is much more impactful—and is way more likely to lead to change—than just telling them they're behaving disrespectfully.

By the way, some people say that coaching sounds a lot like therapy. This is understandable because you're asking people to take a good look at themselves, their attitudes, and behaviors and "own" them. But the primary difference between therapy and coaching is, in therapy you're examining your past to better understand yourself and perhaps free yourself from negative thoughts, feelings,

Coaching Matters

and habits. In coaching, especially during *CfR,* you're examining your language and behaviors, the negative impact they had, and then figuring out what changes you need to make to prevent it from happening again so that you'll have better outcomes. At the same time, you're trying to determine what you respect in the other participants so that you can bear these in mind and leverage them while you're working together in the future.

Your Goal as *CfR* Coach & Facilitator. As the coach and facilitator of the *CfR* process, your goal is to help the participants do the following . . .

1) *Feel that they are in a safe and confidential environment* to the point that they are willing to share their thoughts and feelings.
2) *Acknowledge* the practicality of the three Key Understandings: *"You don't have to like someone to work well with them, but you do have to have some level of respect for them," "It-Takes-Two-To-Tango,"* and *"Who Can I Control? Only Me."*
3) Genuinely *commit to working with you, and the other participant*, on restoring respect to the relationship.
4) *Come to an understanding within themselves,* and agreement with each other, of the "facts" that generated and surrounds the loss of respect, which we refer to as the "what happened," regardless of who is at fault.
5) *Understand their own biases*, communication styles, and "own" their language and behavior that may have contributed to the loss of respect, and most importantly, the impact of these on the other participant.
6) *Develop, internalize and deliver a "Full Apology,"* (if warranted, which it usually is), for their language and behavior before, during, and after the "what happened."
7) *Develop respectful language and behavior* that they are committed to engaging in going forward.
8) *Express the above genuinely* in a joint session.
9) *Come to a mutual agreement* on how they're going to interact with each other, commit to it, and
10) *Engage in the language and behaviors they committed to* during the process and in the joint session.

For tomorrow belongs to the people who prepare for it today.
—African Proverb

Section IV ■
Logistics, Considerations, & Practicalities

Every viable process has some logistics, considerations, and practicalities that support it. In this section, we answer six frequently asked questions around these topics that you may have about facilitating the *CfR* process.

1. *How long does it usually take to run the CfR process?*

Normally, if the participants commit to meeting with you once a week, then after your initial informational meetings with the key stakeholders, the primary coaching/facilitation can be completed in as few as six weeks. This is the optimal time frame and pace. You'll also need some additional weeks for reporting in and following up.

If you compress the process by holding more meetings per week, or completing more steps per meeting, then participants can feel rushed and may become confused or resistant. If you spread the time between meetings out to more than a week or two, the urgency and seriousness of the process may be lost, and it's likely you'll have to take extra time catching participants up on what they said and committed to in previous sessions. There's a rhythm and flow to the process. Once a week with each of the participants usually seems to optimal for everyone and for a successful outcome.

Restoring Respect

Here's how the *CfR* usually rolls out:

Week #	Step #	Actions / Goals	With Whom	Next Meeting In . . .
1	1 & 2	Confirming Understanding, Willingness and Engagement; Explaining the Neuroscience & Some of the "Respect Matters" Concepts	All Stakeholders / The Participants Individually	1 week
2	3 & 4	Obtaining Acknowledgement & Agreement to Go Forward; Begin Administering and Debriefing Assessments & Inquire More About the "what happened."	The Participants Individually	1 week
3 & 4	5 & 6	Coaching Them On Owning Behaviors, Attitudes, and Impacts; Identifying What Is Respected	The Participants Individually	1 week, then 1 week later
5	7 & 8	Determining Wants and Needs, Identifying What Will Change, Gaining Commitment	The Participants Individually	1 week
6	9	Facilitating the Joint Session	The Participants Together	2-6 weeks
8 to 12	10	Reporting Into Stakeholders / Following Up with Check-Ins.	All Stakeholders / The Participants Individually	2x in 2-8 weeks

2. *What should be included in my "Agreement" or Contract with my client?*

You must always have a written and signed contract with your client that clearly lays out the expectations, procedural and compensation agreements, responsibilities, confidentialities, and legal protections between you and your client. We recommend you contact a qualified attorney for assistance with this.

In addition to addressing the items just mentioned, your agreement should also include language that covers these important points:

a) **Intention.** All stakeholders agree that by choosing to engage and participate in the *CfR* process, their overall and genuine intention is to restore some level of respect and reasonable functionality to a specific work relationship.

b) **Voluntary.** All stakeholders, especially the people being coached, are agreeing to participate in the process voluntarily and in good faith, and not because of any coercion, threats, intimidation, or un-disclosed motivations.

c) **Non-Binding.** All stakeholders understand that this process is not a legal or binding remedy, but rather, it is a facilitated conflict and alternative dispute resolution process that does not preclude any other processes or legal remedies that the stakeholders may wish to employ.

d) **Coach Can Shut It Down.** All stakeholders agree that the *CfR* Coach/Facilitator is empowered to shut the process down, at any stage, for any reason and without explanation if they so choose.

e) **No Demands of the Coach.** All stakeholders further agree that they will not attempt to force, insist, or demand that the Coach/Facilitator continue with the process should the Coach/Facilitator decide to shut it down.

f) **Trust & Confidentiality.** All stakeholders understand that the *CfR* process requires a high level of mutual trust and confidentiality from everyone involved and that there should be no expectation by the organization that anything other than general updates on progress will be provided by the *CfR* Coach/Facilitator.

g) **No Guarantees.** The Coach/Facilitator makes no guarantee whatsoever that the process will achieve the desired result and cannot be held responsible if it does not.

h) **Coach Compensation.** All stakeholders agree that the Coach/Facilitator shall be compensated as per their negotiated agreements, regardless of whether the process was fully completed, and/or the outcome.

3. *Should I run the CfR process entirely in person, or on the phone, or using videocalls, or a combination of all three?*

Whenever you're coaching people who are in dispute or conflict, you're going to want to conduct that coaching in person and face-to-face, at first individually, and then together. This allows you to build connection, respect and trust, read their body language and energy, and manage emotionalism more effectively. In person facilitation is vital at the time you bring the participants together toward the end of the *CfR* process.

But, given that so many people are now working remotely, at a huge distance from one another, and/or in hybrid environments, and so many coaches are also working from home, conducting in person, face-to-face sessions may not be practical or even possible. Also, it may not be necessary to conduct in person meetings with the other stakeholders—such as

HR, legal and/or leadership—when a simple phone call or videocall will do.

Here's our recommendation: at the beginning of the engagement, when you're reviewing the process and some of the key concepts with all stakeholders to gain their willingness to have you move forward, holding these meetings via videoconference or a phone call is fine, especially since—if you're external—you may not be formally contracted or on the clock yet. (Note: since the initial steps can take at least a few hours, some external coaches will charge a flat fee or hourly rate for these steps, regardless of whether they move forward with facilitating the overall process.)

When you are under contract and you're specifically coaching the participants who are at the center of the conflict, then conducting the *CfR* process in person is the best option, if possible, especially if they work with each other face-to-face on a regular basis.

The next best option is coaching and facilitating via videocalls, provided that the audio and video quality are good. Videocalls allow you to see facial expressions and body language like head tilts and hand gestures. But, given the sensitivity of the topics being discussed, it's imperative that you insist that the each participant talks with you only when they are alone in a private location, such as a home office with closed doors, where they will not be overheard by colleagues or interrupted (except perhaps momentarily by family or pets). You should never coach anyone who is in a shared space where others may overhear. Although it's not advisable, it is possible to run the entire process through videocalls only—especially when you're working with participants who never see each other in person.

Coaching the *CfR* process over the phone is strongly discouraged; in fact, it's our policy not to do so (although we do provide other types of coaching over the phone).

4. ***What do I need to do to protect myself from being sued?***

Sadly, especially in the US, anytime anyone delivers conflict resolution coaching or facilitates some form of reparative or alternative dispute resolution process or mediation, there's a possibility that the situation will deteriorate and "go legal." This might occur during, or even after a coaching engagement has ended, typically because the participants' employer has engaged in unrelated disciplinary actions, or there's been some perceived retaliation of some kind, and/or people have quit and/or been transferred or demoted or fired.

People who are upset and feel wronged, or companies looking to avoid responsibility, are often looking for others to blame and sue, and you could be one of them. I can tell you from personal experience that being sued—even when you've done nothing wrong—is very stressful to say the least.

Now, if you're an internal coach intending to run the *CfR* process internally, before you start, you're going to want to check with your legal counsel to ensure that you are protected. They may even determine that it's better for all if they run the process themselves or in concert with you, or hire an outsider.

If you're an external coach facilitating *CfR*, you're going to want to have professional insurance. External coaches, advisors, and consultants in the HR arena usually carry general liability insurance along with what's known as, "Errors and Omissions" insurance. E&O insurance is a kind of specialized liability protection against losses not covered by traditional liability insurance. It protects you and your business from claims if a client sues for negligent acts, errors or omissions committed during business activities that result in a financial loss. Many insurers offer E&O insurance to small businesses like one-person coaching firms. Bottom line: if you're doing this work, you'll need to have these types of insurance policies in place.

Also, if you're an external provider, regardless of the kind of coaching or consulting you do, you need a written contract with your clients that has clear disclaimers, confidentiality, liability, and indemnity clauses that offer you protection in the event of a lawsuit. You should have a qualified attorney ensure that your contracts offer you these protections.

One more thought on this topic, if you or your client's corporate counsel have any concerns around your own or their legal exposure, or privilege issues, or frankly, any kind of doubts about the legal issues related to you facilitating the process for them, I strongly recommend that you respectfully decline to move forward, and hand them a copy of this book. Perhaps they'll want to facilitate the process themselves.

5. ***Do I need to have experience in the same industry or business that the people I'm coaching are in?***

Having specific industry experience can help move the process along because won't have to spend time learning about industry processes or jargon.

And many organizations want to hire coaches who have industry experience under the assumption that they already know the territory and will be able to sniff out BS and bad practices expeditiously.

But having experience in your client's industry can also be a hindrance because it's very likely that your experience resulted in you holding specific biases (how could it not?) in favor of, or against certain types of workers or specific practices. This could result in you being less impartial, fair, and evenhanded as you run the *CfR* process.

Sometimes, not knowing anything about the industry, business, or the people you're coaching is a good thing. If you're a quick learner and have had experience coaching people in a range of industries, then not having specific industry experience is not going to take up a lot of extra time. In fact, you may be able to use it to your advantage; you can "play dumb" for example, asking people to explain industry specifics to you while you're listening for their biases, their attitudes around respect, and any coloring around the "what happened."

When a company is looking to hire an outsider to help them with a workplace conflict matter, they *should* be looking for someone who is an expert in workplace conflict and not just an expert in their industry. Too many times we've seen industry experts, with little or no training in coaching, alternative dispute resolution techniques, or mediation, wade into an emotionally charged situation and make it worse. When it comes to restoring respect in the workplace, when in doubt, hire an expert in running the *CfR* process.

6. ***How will I know that I need to shut down the process before it's completed?***

There are many factors and behaviors that may cause you to shut down the *CfR* process before completion. It can be as much a gut call as it is a rational, logical decision. But—as agreed to in writing by all stakeholders—it is your call to make. Of course, your client's leadership or HR could shut you down for whatever reason, but that's out of your control.

Here are some "red flags," to look for that could lead you to halt the process and shut it down before completion:

a) **Unrightable Wrong.** One or both participants is consistently adamant over the course of more than one coaching session that the other has engaged in an "unrightable wrong," they they've permanently lost respect for them, and that no apology or behavioral change will make any difference.

b) **It's Not Me.** One or both participants is consistently adamant over the course of more than one coaching session that they have done nothing wrong; that they believe the other participant is at fault for the loss of respect, or the other participant is too sensitive, doesn't have the right, or has no basis for a complaint, or is attempting to undermine their role, project and/or career.

c) **Coercion.** One or both participants, at any point in the process, express-es that they felt forced, coerced, or manipulated into participating; and/or that they believe their employer implied that their participation is a condition of employment; and/or they expressed that they wouldn't go through the process if they'd believed they had a choice.

d) **Stalling.** Typically, the primary coaching (not including the Reporting In/Follow Up) can be completed in six weeks, which is the optimal time frame for the *CfR* process. If one or both of the participants claim they're too busy to meet for 60-90 minutes once per week, or that their schedule demands that the process must be spread out over the course of many months, or cancels more than one meeting at the last minute, it's more than likely that they're stalling because they don't consider the matter to be very serious or urgent, and/or that they would prefer to avoid emo-tional discussions or talking about the "what happened," and their role in it, and/or they have little or no respect for the other participant, the process, you, or their organization.

e) **Stakeholder Out of Integrity.** You get the impression before or during the process that the other stakeholders (HR, legal, leadership) have al-ready determined another course of action (such as discipline, demo-tion, transfer, or termination), and are simply using the CfR process as a "cover-our-backsides" maneuver and/or as part of an affirmative defense in the event of a lawsuit. Though not illegal, doing this lacks integrity and could put you at greater risk in the event of a lawsuit (although that risk is always there). It means that they aren't necessarily supportive of the possibility that the two participants can restore respect through the *CfR* process and are simply making it an exercise in protecting the organization. This is something you probably don't want to be a part of because when people operate out if integrity, things tend to go badly and innocent people get swept up into the mess.

f) **Damaging Information Revealed.** During the process, one or both participants reveals information that could be damaging to the organization in some way, or reveals personal issues or physical or mental health challenges that could undermine or derail the process, or threatens the other participants and/or the organization with physical, financial, legal, or emotional harm. In any of these cases, you should shut the process down, and report these to your client, preferably to their legal counsel to protect confidentiality.

g) **Loss of Willingness.** During the process, one or both participants feels they are unable to continue and cannot be coached otherwise. They may fear retaliation, be overwhelmed emotionally, don't want to take responsibility for their role in the "what happened," or have come to realize that they don't want to commit to changing their behavior going forward.

If any of these red flags present themselves and become impediments to progress despite your best efforts to coach the participants past them, then you will need to shut the *CfR* process down, just as you promised the stakeholders you would. Then, it is up to them to determine their next steps.

The Ten Steps of the
Coaching for Respect™ Process

Step One: **Confirming Understanding, Willingness, & Engagement** - *PAGE 59*
Informational Meetings with All Stakeholders and Individual Participants

Step Two: **Explaining the Neuroscience and Respect Matters** - *PAGE 63*
Informational Meetings with Individual Participants

Step Three: **Obtaining Formal Understanding, Willingness to Go Forward** - *PAGE 69*
Meetings with Individual Participants to Obtain Formal Buy-In,
Initiating Assessments

Step Four: **Debriefing Assessments and Conducting Findings of Fact** - *PAGE 71*
Helping Participants Understand Their Assessments, Learning More About
the "What Happened"

Step Five: **Coaching Individually—Owning Behaviors, Attitudes, & Impacts** - *PAGE 75*
Coaching the Participants on Greater Self-Awareness

Step Six: **Identifying What Is Respected** - *PAGE 81*
Coaching the Participants on What They Respect in Each Other

Step Seven: **Determining Wants and Needs** - *PAGE 85*
Determining What Each Participant Wants and Needs from the Other

Step Eight: **Identifying What Will Change, Gaining Commitment** - *PAGE 89*
Coaching Them on Developing Change Lists

Step Nine: **Facilitating the Joint Session** - *PAGE 97*
Facilitating the Seven Phases of the Joint Session

Step Ten: **Reporting In/Following Up** - *PAGE 113*
Reporting in to Stakeholders, Conducting Check-In Calls

Coaches and the people they coach know that for the future to be different,
we need to change the way we do things in the present. More often, changes
involve shifts in attitudes, thinking, perceptions, and behavior.
—Gary Collins

Coaching for Respect™
Step One

Confirming Understanding, Willingness and Engagement

Step One Goals: *Ensure that all stakeholders understand . . .*

A. What the *CfR* process is and how it rolls out

B. That it's voluntary for the participants and separate from other actions the organization might take

C. That your role is "Coach / Facilitator"

D. That the overall goal is to restore respect to the relationship

E. Some of the concepts around respect that are in play

F. That it's not guaranteed to work; that success is in the hands of the participants and their willingness to engage and restore respect to the relationship

G. That you will shut it down if you believe people, and/or the organization are out of integrity

Time It Takes: *2-4 hours with all participants and stakeholders*

Restoring Respect

Overview. This first step takes place after you've had initial conversations with your prospective client's HR or legal folks, in which you discussed the possibility of employing the *CfR* process in their organization, and perhaps sent them a written process description, outline, timeframe, and goals.

In Step One, you'll be conducting meetings with all stakeholders, including HR, legal, leadership, and individually with the participants who have fallen out of respect for each other, to explain the *CfR* process, how it works, the timeframes, some of the key concepts involved, and to gauge their willingness to have you run the process.

During this step, it's also very likely that you'll start hearing stories of "what happened," from each stakeholder's perspective, as well as information regarding previous incidents, and about the perceptions, interests, organizational politics, and the sense of urgency that this situation be resolved.

You should be aware that this step focuses primarily on providing information to all the stakeholders, especially the people who've lost respect for each other and who will be directly coached throughout. You're not yet facilitating or coaching, you're informing and explaining, and doing a lot of listening and information gathering.

But, when you're explaining the process, it's important keep focused on the overall definition and what it's going to take to get it done.

NOTE: In each step, I'll provide you with suggestions as to the language you can use and the things you can say. It's essentially a script that you can follow. We call these "Words You Can Use."

Step One

Step One—Words You Can Use. (Things you can actually say).

About The Process. The *CfR* process is designed to support the participants in restoring some level of respect to their relationship to the point where they can work together effectively going forward. It's strictly voluntary, and it uses various techniques, including workplace relationship coaching, psychology, mediation, interpersonal communication facilitation, and alternative dispute resolution.

Coach's Role. My role is to guide the participants through the process, ask questions that may uncover and challenge perceptions, and to ensure everyone remains in integrity throughout. As the coach, if I conclude that someone is acting out of integrity or is no longer willing to go forward, and despite my best coaching they won't change their minds, or if the organization does something to undermine the process, then I will call a halt to it and shut it down. We will need to formally agree at the outset that I have the authority to do this.

How Long It Takes. Typically, once everyone has committed to going forward, the process rolls out in four-to-six private, individual 60-90 minute coaching sessions over four-to-six weeks. Eventually, I bring the participants together for a joint session that may run 1-3 hours. Although conducting the process in person is best, we can do it via videoconference if we must.

No Guarantees. Success is not guaranteed, and it really depends on the people being coached: if they're participating voluntarily, if they genuinely want to restore the relationship to functionality, and if they're willing to look at their own behavior, and possibly apologize for it, regardless of whether it was intentional or not. They'll also be asked to make commitments to themselves and to each other on how they are going to behave going forward. Again, all of this is voluntary and depends on the willingness of participants to do the work.

Organizational Support. Success also depends on the organization's integrity and willingness to allow this process to go forward without interfering. If it's being employed only as an affirmative defense in the event of a lawsuit, then that's out of integrity, and the process should not move forward. If it's being used as an excuse not to directly address repeated bad behavior that everyone's known about for some time, then that's out of integrity too and the process should not move forward. And if the organization intends to micro-manage me as I facilitate, then I will sense that and will very likely call a halt.

Step One—Words You Can Use. Checklist: Ask the Stakeholders . . .

☐ Are you aware that the primary goal of the *CfR* process is to restore some level of respect between the participants to the point where they can function effectively as co-workers going forward?

☐ Do you understand how the process works, that it is voluntary, and separate and distinct from investigative and disciplinary processes and other legal remedies?

☐ Do you understand that this process is not a legal or binding remedy, but rather, it is a facilitated conflict and alternative dispute resolution technique that does not preclude any other disciplinary processes or legal remedies?

☐ Are you aware that the *CfR* process is not guaranteed to work, and that success primarily depends on the participants' willingness to be coached and the integrity to see it through?

☐ As HR/Legal/Leadership, can you assure me that the participants involved aren't being forced, manipulated, or coerced to participate in any way or as a "condition of employment?"

☐ As HR/Legal/Leadership, can you assure me that you won't attempt to micro-manage or undermine the process and that you are not solely using the process to provide the organization with an affirmative defense in the event of a lawsuit.

☐ Do you understand, acknowledge, and confirm that I have the authority to pause or stop the process at any time and disengage completely if I sense that one or both of the participants, or any of the stakeholders, are out of integrity or attempting to manipulate, undermine, or force the process to a conclusion one way or another?

☐ Will you—as the person being coached—confirm that you are voluntarily participating in this process, that you aren't being forced or coerced to participate, and that there's been no implication of negative consequences if you don't?

☐ Are you aware that this process requires a great deal of trust and confidentiality and therefor it is unlikely that I will be providing HR/Legal/Leadership with any detailed progress reports beyond, "we're in the process," "the process has been halted permanently," or "the process has been completed"?

☐ Are you, after being advised of all the above, willing to commit in writing to move forward with the *CfR* process?

We are not thinking beings who happen to be emotional;
we are emotional beings who happen to think.
—Joseph LeDoux, Neuroscientist

Coaching for Respect™
Step Two

Explaining the Neuroscience of Respect and Disrespect,
& Some of the "Respect Matters" Concepts

Step Two Goals: *Ensure the Participants . . .*

Are briefed on all the steps of the *CfR* process, and on what's expected of them in each step to the point that you are assured they understand what they're committing to.

  A. Have some general understanding of the Neuroscience of Respect and disrespect and some of the interpersonal dynamics that will come into play while attempting to restore respect to their working relationship.

  B. Are genuinely interested in restoring respect to their working relationship.

  C. Are voluntarily participating and are not being coerced or forced or manipulated.

  D. Are not immovably convinced that the other has engaged in an "unrightable wrong," or has no basis or right to complain (thus rendering the process a waste of time), or if they are, then . . .

  E. Are at least genuinely willing to explore the possibility—however remote—that some level of respect can be restored and the relationship repaired to the point where it functions reasonably well, at least from a business point of view.

F. Have received a copy of the *Statement of Understanding and Willingness (S.U.W.)* and are committed to reviewing it and the process and inform you of their decision to participate, or not, prior to or during the next meeting (in approximately one week).

G. Are introduced to any assessments you may be using, such as the DISC.

Time It Takes: *30-60 minutes per person being coached*

Overview. During this step (which can happen at the same time as Step One), you are meeting individually with the people being coached who have lost respect for each other and focusing on the foundational concepts found in Section 1 | Respect Matters. These include the Neuroscience of Respect, *"You don't have to like . . . but you do have to have some level of respect," "It-Takes-Two-To-Tango,"* and *"Who Can I Change? Only Me,"* among others. You'll also be introducing the concept of the *"unrightable wrong,"* how that may play a role, or not, in the process, and gauging if you're working with someone who is genuinely willing to engage.

You should also outline the *CfR* process very clearly, so that each participant understands what's going to happen, when it's going to happen, and what will be expected of them. You'll be giving them a copy of the *Statement of Understanding and Willingness* to read through and consider prior to your next meeting.

Like Step One, Step Two is mostly informational. But, with their permission you can start administering assessments. You'll also want to start generating the possibility in the participants' minds that there are primitive physiological responses to respect and disrespect that they might not be aware of, that not every incidence of disrespect is intentional, and that feelings of respect and disrespect are just that, feelings, and not necessarily the result of rational, cognitive thought.

As you move through Step Two, you're getting a better idea of the "what happened," its impact on the participants and their team or organization, and whether you think respect can be restored to the relationship to the point where they can work together reasonably well.

Step Two

In Step Two, you'll need to ramp up your listening skills and pay close attention to your instincts, because it's likely you may hear or learn of something that triggers a red flag (see Section IV). If it does, unless it's truly egregious to the point of crossing a policy or legal line, hold off on deciding whether to go forward, until after you complete this step. And, if you do sense potential red flags, you should be transparent, and inform the participants and anyone else who triggers a red flag that you have concerns and how these may lead you to shut the process down.

Step Two—Checklist: Inform the Participants . . .

☐ About the *Coaching for* Respect™ process, general timeframes and expectations around willingness and integrity.

☐ About the Neuroscience of Respect and Disrespect.

☐ About the Assessments you may be using.

☐ About the concepts, *"You don't have to like, but . . . " "It-Takes-Two-To-Tango,"* and *"Who Can I Control?"*

☐ That you need to hear from them the "what happened" that led to the loss of respect, any related backstory and incidents, and their perspective on it all. That you're listening for "gunnysacking," and mentions of what could be an "unrightable wrong."

☐ About the "unrightable wrong," (this is critical). f you hear one or both participants speaking in absolutes, i.e., "I want nothing to do with them," "What they did was inexcusable," "There's no way I would want to work with them again," and/or repeated expressions of loathing, disgust, and contempt for the other.

(Note: an expression of loathing or disgust for the other's *behavior*—as separate from the person—is not necessarily an indicator that restoring respect to the relationship is impossible.)

☐ (Toward the end of this step), About Red Flags you're listening for that may lead you to shut the process down.

Restoring Respect

☐ About the *Statement of Understanding and Willingness (S.U.W.)* that they will need to sign (typically during the second meeting with the participants).

☐ That you'll be giving them approximately one week to consider everything and that before or during the next meeting, if they wish to participate, that they'll need to commit by signing the *S.U.W.*, or inform you that they are not willing to move forward.

(The following page should be printed out separately and given to the participants for their review.)

Statement of Understanding & Willingness (S.U.W.)

By signing below I'm indicating that the Coach/Facilitator has explained the CfR process, and I have read the following: (please check each box and then sign)

☐ **A.** I understand how the *Coaching for Respect*™ process works, the effort and commitment required of me to participate, as well as the concepts around respect and disrespect as explained to me by the Coach/Facilitator.

☐ **B.** I understand that my participation is entirely voluntary and that I'm choosing to do so willingly because I genuinely wish to have a productive working relationship with the other participants once the process is complete.

☐ **C.** I understand that any assessments that may be used are confidential and will not be shared with my organization or other participants without my expressed consent.

☐ **D.** I understand that this process is separate and distinct from other actions, processes, and remedies my organization may choose to undertake regarding the "what happened," and any related incidents or behaviors that led to this process becoming an option.

☐ **E.** I have not been forced, coerced, or otherwise required to participate.

☐ **F.** I understand that the Coach/Facilitator will not be sharing the content of our discussions with anyone without the written consent of all participants.

☐ **G**. I understand that the Coach/Facilitator may choose to shut down the process at any time for any number of reasons.

☐ **H.** I may inform the Coach/Facilitator at any time that I am no longer willing to participate in the process, but I am willing to discuss the reasons why, and that I may or may not change my mind.

☐ **I.** I understand that the *Coaching for Respect*™ process, when completed, is not guaranteed to result in a functional working relationship between me and the other participant.

☐ **J.** I understand the process requires trust and confidentiality, and I agree not to share the content of our discussions without the written consent of the Coach/Facilitator and other participant.

☐ **K.** I will make a good-faith effort to stay in the process, complete it and move forward in a respectful working relationship with the other participant.

Signed_____ Name/Date _____

Signed_____ Name/Date _____

Coach/Facilitator's Signature_____

Name/Date _____

*The willingness to show up changes us, it makes us
a little braver each time.*
—Brené Brown

Coaching for Respect™
Step Three

Obtaining Formal Understanding & Willingness to Go Forward

Step Three Goals:

A. Ensure the participants understand what they're committing to (by reviewing with them the *Statement of Understanding and Willingness*).

B. Ensure neither participant is being coerced, forced, or manipulated to participate.

C. Ensure the participants understand what being "in integrity" with the process means, (i.e., being open to coaching, honesty, genuine willingness to own your own behavior and apologize for it, willingness to identify and commit to behaviors that enable the relationship to be productive going forward, etc.)

D. Ensure neither participant is convinced that an "unrightable wrong" has occurred or that the other participant has no basis or right to complain. Or, if they believe otherwise, then ensure that they are genuinely willing to explore the possibility that respect can be restored.

E. Begin Debriefing Assessments (if you haven't already).

F. Inquire more about the "what happened."

Time It Takes: *10-20 minutes per participant*

Restoring Respect

Overview. Typically, Step Three occurs during the second individual meetings between you and the people who've lost respect for each other, after they've had some time (typically a week) to think it all through and to review the *Statement of Understanding & Willingness* that you provided them in Step Two.

All this ensuring and re-ensuring may seem like overkill, especially if the participants keep saying "yes," and "let's get on with it." The thing of it is, once you get deep into the "what happened," their role in it, and the language and behaviors they evinced, and their impact on others, they might start wishing they hadn't pushed to move forward so quickly. It's at that point you'll remind them of what they agreed to in writing and urge them to stay with it, as they promised.

Once you've reviewed the above and the participants have signed the S.U.W., you can provide the links and instructions to any assessments you might use (DISC, etc.) and if there's time, ask more questions on the "what happened."

We cannot change what we are not aware of,
and once we are aware, we cannot help but change.
—Sheryl Sandberg

Coaching for Respect™
Step Four

Debriefing Assessments & Conducting Findings of Fact

Step Four Goals: *to get a clearer understanding of . . .*

A. The communication styles, and perhaps the personalities, of the participants involved using assessments.

B. The "what happened" from each person's perspective.

C. The facts that are not in dispute and any that still are.

D. Whether or not there is a pattern of similar behavior in the past either with each other or others.

E. How the participants felt about it all.

F. How the participants changed their behavior (if they did) as a result of the incident(s).

G. Whether or not there are any "unrightable wrongs" that have cropped up.

H. How the participants think and feel about respect in general.

Time It Takes: *varies per participant*

Restoring Respect

Overview. In this step, which can take place during the same session as Step Three if you have the time, you're administering, analyzing, and debriefing assessments as a way of helping the participants gain some understanding of their own and others' styles and perspectives. Our recommended assessments for the *CfR* process are the *DISC Communication Styles* and the *Emotional Intelligence Quotient-2*. There are many, many others that may prove helpful to you in facilitating the process such as the *Thomas-Kilmann Conflict Mode Instrument* (TKI), and *The Hogan Personality Inventory.*

If you use assessments, then you know how valuable they can be in giving you a better sense of the people you're coaching and how they may be aligned or in conflict with each other. Of course, you can run the *CfR* process without using assessments, but it may take longer and the potential for misunderstanding and miscommunication is greater.

Once they've taken the assessments, you'll be able to debrief with the participants individually and point out the differences between them. For example, someone who is all about solving problems and focusing on tasks and who doesn't see the importance of respect could be unaware that in their drive to achieve they have run roughshod over someone who believes that good working relationships lead to great outcomes and that being respected by a colleague is the key to working well with them. It's entirely possible that these two people perceive each other as disrespectful: the first may be thinking that the second is wasting their time with relationship stuff and the second may be thinking the first is being rude and insensitive.

Knowing their style and priority differences can, at the very least, help the participants better understand why the other participant does what they do and says what they say. This mutual understanding can also help you bring the temperature down between them and begin the drive toward identifying behaviors that need to change.

You'll also be asking questions to gauge how the participants feel about respect in general and exploring their expectations around respectful behaviors (such as, "one must always respect your elders/those in authority," etc.).

And, of course, you'll also continue, as you have in the previous steps, to ask questions about facts and perceptions around the "what happened."

By the way, this fact-finding mission could involve talking to witnesses, colleagues, etc. provided the participants give you permission. But broadening the fact-finding beyond the participants is problematic. Not only does it increase the risk of others learning about the "what happened," and taking sides, it also

Step Four

starts to publicize the incident(s) and the fact that people are going through the *CfR* process. This could make facilitating the process that much more difficult for all the participants involved. Remember, this is not a formal "investigation," so the fewer people involved directly in the process, the better.

As for finding facts and determining perceptions of the other participants, we developed a quick exercise that helps you move this step along.

Exercise: the "What Happened"

Ask your participant to write down the answers to the following questions as specifically as they can . . .

1. What do you remember from the incident(s) in terms of who said and did what and in what sequence.

2. What were the feelings you experienced at the time, i.e., *anger, shock, humiliation, frustration, disappointment, surprise, etc.* (these are all commonly used descriptors by those who feel disrespected), and *wasn't aware, surprised, confused, pity, disgust, uninterested, don't care, embarrassed for them, frustrated, just wanted to move on* (these are all commonly used descriptors by those who have been Accused of being disrespectful).

3. After the incident in question, did your opinion of the other person change? If so, how?

4. Did you change your own behavior? If so, how?

5. Where there any other incidents involving this person that were like this?

Coaching for Respect™
Step Five

Coaching Them Individually—Owning Behaviors, Attitudes, and Impacts

Step Five Goals.

A. To support the participants, individually, in identifying and examining their own behaviors and attitudes during the "what happened," and previously.

B. To coach them to "own" any of their behaviors and attitudes that were reported to be disrespectful or perceived to have a negative impact on others.

C. To coach them to identify the negative impacts of their behaviors on others.

D. To remind the participants of the concept, "*It-Takes-Two-To-Tango*," when it comes to restoring respect to a work relationship.

Time It Takes: *30-60 minutes per participant*

Overview. In this step, you're focusing on identifying the language and behaviors that occurred during the "what happened" that the participants are willing to admit to and "own." You're also trying to understand *why* they said or did it, and the impact it may have had on others including the team, division, organization, and customers, etc.

Restoring Respect

It's important to note that there are at least four different "actors" in this drama, each with their own perceptions of the "what happened" and its impact. Unfortunately, the labels we use for them, while convenient, have the ring of legality to them:

1. Aggrieved—*someone who feels disrespected*
2. Accused—*someone who's been accused of behaving disrespectfully*
3. bystanders—*others who heard or saw the language and behaviors*
4. stakeholders—*others who are aware of the "what happened" and are either impacted directly, indirectly, and/or have a stake in the outcome.*

If you're coaching someone who has been accused of being disrespectful, you're more than likely going to face some defensiveness, shifting of blame, surprise, trivialization, or denial. Your coaching job in this step is to help de-escalate them to the point where they'll set their emotions aside, admit what they did or said and offer a reasonable assessment on how it may have hurt or negatively impacted others. You'll get to "what needs to change" later in the process.

If you're coaching the Aggrieved person—the person who feels disrespected—typically they'll be very forthcoming and clear about the "what happened," and the things the Accused said or did that they perceived as disrespectful.

You may also find that the Aggrieved person is defensive when you ask them if they did or said anything disrespectful themselves. They may claim that they didn't do anything wrong, and it's all the other participant's fault, etc. This is where you may need to remind them about the *Neuroscience of Respect*; that we go into fight, flight, freeze mode when we feel disrespected and may inadvertently and unintentionally say or do things that make the situation worse. You can also remind them that the *It-Takes-Two-To-Tango* concept, in addition to being one of the keys to the *CfR* process, also applies to most working relationships where the participants need to cooperate and collaborate—aka, do the work dance—in order to get things done.

As for the bystanders, if there are any, if they're asked about the "what happened," they may have any number of reactions and perceptions, including the Aggrieved is "too sensitive," the Accused was "definitely disrespectful," "both were disrespectful," the incident is "being overblown," or it's just the "tip of the iceberg." Also, their loyalties may be complex: to the Aggrieved, to the Accused, to the team, the organization or expectations around respect and any combination of these to varying degrees. This can be complicated!

Step Five

So, work hard to keep your eye focused on the goal of this step: *to coach each person to explore, uncover, admit, and own any of their language and behaviors that may have been perceived as disrespectful by others and to understand how others may have been negatively impacted.* You'll know you're doing a good job when people are saying, "Yes, I did/said that, and I can see how others perceived it as disrespectful."

Handling Defensiveness. During this step, almost all the participants are going to be defensive to some degree, even the Aggrieved. We've found the best way to deescalate, reduce defensiveness and have people own their behavior is to use a method we developed here at the Center for Respectful Leadership, called O.D.P. (or ODP[2]).

O—Obtain Openness
D—Decrease Defensiveness
P—Promote Possibility

Obtain Openness. One of the easiest ways to get someone to open up about their own behavior and attitudes is to ask them open-ended questions in a way that demonstrates that you're genuinely curious, that you really want to know and understand without seeming to be judgmental. Here are some examples of questions you can ask:

Words You Can Use.

- "So that I can understand what happened better, would you be willing to take me through the incident as it rolled out, making sure you describe everything everyone said or did, including you?"

- "Would you be able to describe the incident and the behaviors and language that you felt were disrespectful?"

- "Do you think others would perceive this as disrespectful too?"

- "What were the feelings you had during and after the incident?"

- "If you're being Accused of being disrespectful, setting aside whether you think what you did/said was disrespectful and setting aside your intentions, what do you *think* they're talking about? Or what do you *think* is at the core of their complaint?"

- "How did you perceive your relationship before this occurred?"

- "Can you help me understand what you were thinking when you said/did that?"

- "I'm wondering what was going on in your head at that time?"

Decrease Defensiveness. Most of us, when we're accused of being disrespectful, will get somewhat defensive, that's only human. As a coach, it's hard to get someone to admit and own their negative behavior if they've put up a shield around themselves. One of the best ways to decrease defensiveness is to tell the person what you and others respect in them, for example:

Words You Can Use.

- "I respect your willingness to dig into this uncomfortable topic."

- "It's my sense that you are respected at this organization for your _____ (*knowledge & experience, talents, and skills,* and/or *the way you treat others*).

- "I understand that it wasn't your intention for them to feel disrespected."

- "If it was your intention to be disrespectful, in hindsight what do you think of the result? Is this the best possible outcome?"

- "I think you wouldn't go through this process if you didn't have some respect for the other participants."

Promote Possibilities. Once you've gained the participants' openness to talk about their own behavior and language, decreased their defensiveness, and gotten them to admit and "own" what they said and did, you'll need to coach them to consider the possibility that others could feel disrespected by it and that these feelings are legitimate. You might take this opportunity to remind them of the *Who Can I Control? Only Me* concept here, by saying something like, "As you remember, we can't control what others think or do. If they feel disrespected, they feel disrespected, and that's that." Here are some of the things you can ask that will help you promote possibilities:

Words You Can Use.

With the Accused . . .

- "Think back to an incident in your own life when you felt disrespected. Did anyone tell you that you were overreacting? If they did, how did you feel about them saying that to you?"

- "When you feel strongly about something and someone trivializes it or says you're overreacting, how do you react?"

- "Aren't we all entitled to feel however we feel?"

- "How likely are you to change how you feel about someone's behavior just because they told you that you should?"

- "If the roles were reversed and the other participants in this process treated you in a way that you personally find disrespectful, what impact might that have on you and your relationship with them going forward?"

- "Is it possible that the person who feels disrespected actually has a legitimate point of view?"

With the Aggrieved . . .

- "Even though they behaved disrespectfully, is it possible that the Accused (use actual name) found the way you responded to be disrespectful to them?"

- "If so, would you be willing to admit that you've been disrespectful?"

Restoring Respect

- "If yes, then how do you think your behavior impacted them? If no, then can you understand why they might not want to admit and own their own behavior?"

- "Aren't we all entitled to feel however we feel?"

- "Given the *It-Takes-Two-To-Tango* concept, can you see that relationships are not completely one-sided and that both participants need to be mindful of their behavior and language?"

As we grow as unique persons, we learn to
respect the uniqueness of others.
—Robert Schuller

Coaching for Respect™
Step Six

Identifying What Is Respected

Step Six Goals. *Ensure that . . .*

A. Each participant identified at least one, if not two or more traits/attributes, etc. in the other participant that they genuinely respect.

B. They understand that what they respect does, in some way, play a role in the work that they do together. Ideally, it would be knowledge and experience, or talents and skills that are so critical, and that without them neither would be able to do their jobs.

C. They understand the "Homework" assignment—see below.

Time It Takes: *30-60 minutes per participant*

Overview. This step often takes place during the same session as Step Five, typically toward the end. This is arguably the most important step in the CfR process, in which you are encouraging the participants to identify the traits and attributes that they respect in the other person.

Often a participant might say to you, "After what's happened, I really don't like this person anymore." This is understandable, but it's at this point that you'll remind them of what we at the Center for Respectful Leadership call "The Big Idea," which reads . . . *You Don't Have to Like Someone to Work With Them, But You Do Have to Have Some Level of Respect for Them.*

As I mentioned in Section II, *Respect Matters*, typically what we respect in our work colleagues falls into these three areas, or attributes:

- Knowledge and experience (and position attained as a result)
- Talents and skills, and/or
- The way they treat us and others.

By having each person identify what they respect in the other, they start to break down hardened perceptions, such as the Aggrieved person only seeing the Accused through a lens called "disrespectful person," while the Accused only seeing the Aggrieved through a lens called "too sensitive," and "complainer."

This is one of the most difficult steps to move through because strong feelings about the other participant's behavior may cause someone to be very resistant to seeing them in anything but a negative light. You're going to have to work hard here and be persistent, respectfully of course!

Ideally, you're trying to get them to identify something they respect that relates to their work *together*. For example, the Aggrieved respects a particular skill that the Accused has, and understands that without it being utilized, their own work will be much harder, or impossible, to accomplish.

You need to be aware that the Accused, who may be trying to downplay their role in the "what happened," and curry favor with you, might have been stipulating throughout that they've always had some level of respect for the Aggrieved, that a mountain is being made from a molehill, and they'd like to just get this whole process done and over with so they can get back to work.

If you're hearing language like this, and sensing resentment or resignation as the Accused tells you what they respect in the Aggrieved, then you'll need to be careful: it could be they don't really respect the Aggrieved, they just want to get the process over with and done.

To ensure that the Accused is being genuine, ask them to specifically name the traits and attributes they respect in the Aggrieved, and provide you with specific examples of events, times, and places where the Aggrieved elicited and engaged in behaviors and language that the Accused respects. Then confirm those events with the Aggrieved, that they really happened, and whether they felt respect from the Accused at the time. If there's alignment between the two, it's likely the Accused is being honest about what they respect in the Aggrieved.

As for the Aggrieved, because they feel disrespected and now that the whole situation has been emotionally elevated by the fact that they are involved in the *CfR* process, they may struggle to define what they respect in the Accused. You'll need to remind them of the nature of intent, and that it's entirely possible the Accused did not intend to disrespect them and that even though they did, they may have other traits and attributes that can be respected.

Make sure to acknowledge any strong feelings that the Aggrieved has, that they are legitimate, and that you're not trying to minimize the "what happened." You're simply trying to determine if there are traits and attributes that the Aggrieved respects in the Accused. Often this distinction can be helpful.

A word of caution: do not accept *"there's nothing I respect in them,"* as their final answer, because if you do, you literally won't be able to move forward with the process, and you'll have to shut it down. As you know, without some level of respect for co-worker, it's almost impossible to work effectively and productively with them. Here are some approaches and opening lines you might use:

Words You Can Use.

- "What would you say the organization values in the other person?"

- "Typically, organizations try to leverage people's knowledge and experience, and their talents and skills to get things done and accomplish business goals. Is there anything that you know about the other participant that falls into these categories and which the organization is leveraging successfully?"

- "Have you had any firsthand experience with the other participant where you became aware that they were doing what you would consider quality work?

- "If so, what was it?"

- "Do you have colleagues whom you respect and who you think have respect for the other participant in this process?"

- "If so, then what do you think your colleagues respect in the other participant?"

- "Looking at the other participant's knowledge and experience, or talents and skills, is there anything that you do respect? Be specific."

- "Can you point to specific events where the other participant engaged in behaviors that you consider respectful? If so, what were they?"

- "If you could set aside the 'what happened' and your feelings about it for a moment, is there anything about them that you would say you had some level of respect for, such as their knowledge and experience or talents and skills?"

One thing you'll need to listen carefully for is one or both saying: "*I respect them for (XYZ), but they (disrespected me/I feel disrespected)."* The "but" indicates that their negative feelings around the "what happened" are overriding the traits and attributes that they do respect and may be an indication that they believe an "unrightable wrong" has occurred. If this is the case then this is where you'll be doing your most nuanced and persistent coaching: you must determine if this person has enough respect for the other that they are open to working with them going forward *if* certain conditions are met, which is where Step Seven comes into play.

Homework. Occasionally, you'll need to assign homework to your participants, i.e., things to consider between coaching sessions. This is one of those times you're definitely assigning homework.

Once the participants have identified what they respect in the other, assign them the following:

"Before our next session, I want to you to consider what you need and want from the other participant that will make it possible for you to start working with them again in a way that is productive, effective and without the tension that the 'what happened' has generated. Don't answer this question now. Please think about it carefully and come prepared to discuss at our next session."

You think you know what you want and how it's all supposed to turn out.
When all is said and done, you get what you need.
—Kate McGahan

Coaching for Respect™
Step Seven

Determining Wants and Needs

Step Seven Goals. *Determine . . .*

A. What each participant Wants and Needs from the other(s) to feel that they can work effectively and productively with them without the tension that the "what happened" generated.

B. What their specific Wants and Needs are in terms of what they want the other to do rather than in what they want the other to stop doing (examples below).

C. Modification of their Wants and Needs in terms of ensuring that they are reasonable and achievable by the other person.

Time It Takes: *15-30 minutes per participant*

Overview. This step usually occurs during session five. Once you've reached this point in the process, the participants should have acknowledged that they have some level of respect for some traits or attributes of the other. They've also done their "homework," by thinking about what they want and need to work productively and effectively going forward without the tension that the "what happened," generated.

Restoring Respect

Typically, the Accused doesn't want and need much from the Aggrieved, other than perhaps a commitment to let bygones be bygones and to get back to work. At this point, you can accept this response. But don't worry, you aren't letting the Accused off the hook. In Step Eight, you'll be asking them directly to identify what they are willing to change and do going forward that will ensure the relationship will be productive and effective.

As for the Aggrieved person, during this step, they're usually very clear about what they want and need from the Accused. In my experience, they started mentioning these needs in the very first coaching session. I make note of them and say, "We'll get to those later in the process."

Wants and Needs of the Aggrieved. Almost always, the Aggrieved will indicate that they need: a sincere and genuine apology from the Accused in which they clearly . . .

- "Own" what they said and did
- Acknowledge how it negatively impacted the Aggrieved (and others and the organization).
- Commit to not to do it again, and . . .
- Going forward, to behave differently, in specific ways that ensure that it, and other disrespectful behaviors don't happen again.

Essentially, the Aggrieved needs what we at the Center for Respectful Leadership call a Full Apology from the Accused before they're willing to consider putting in the effort to work effectively and productively with them again. This is entirely normal and understandable. You'll find the Full Apology process in Step Eight.

Sometimes the Aggrieved doesn't want a "Full Apology," and that's acceptable. But you'll want to press them on what they need to specifically see and hear from the Accused for them to feel comfortable moving forward with the relationship.

Coach them to express these as, "Please do this," and "Please do that." Or, if they feel that they must insist the Accused stop doing something, then they need to identify what they want them to do instead. This is because, as human beings, it's hard for us to just stop doing something because somebody else requires it of us, or we require it of ourselves. Usually, we need to replace the problematic behavior with good or at least, acceptable behavior.

Step Seven

To get your participants to be specific, you might want to offer the following examples:

- "To me, being given orders and commands feels disrespectful. Saying 'please,' and 'thank you' sincerely works for me."
- "Instead of interrupting me during meetings, please make a note of what you need to say and say it when I'm finished speaking."
- "Instead of making disparaging comments about me and our co-workers, please say something good about them, or about something you value or respect in them. Or say nothing at all."
- "Instead of doing what I consider to be micro-managing me, let's agree together on what's expected of me using SMART goals, and then it's up to me to achieve them; and then you can hold me accountable to them."

One last note about Wants and Needs. Sometimes one or both are so angry or upset that their wants and needs are unrealistic. For example, "I never want to speak with them again," or "they're only allowed to speak to me when they have a specific work-related request. Otherwise, I don't want to interact with them at all." These are unreasonable and frankly, in most cases, unworkable. You'll have to coach the person in understanding why a particular need or want is unreasonable and support them in modifying them.

Once you have commitment, you need the discipline and
hard work to get you there.
—Haile Gebrselassie

Coaching for Respect™
Step Eight

Identifying What Will Change, Gaining Commitment

Goals for Step Eight:

A. Prepare the participants for the joint session by explaining what is going to occur and reminding them of some of the core concepts of respect.

B. Teach the techniques of a Full Apology, Reflective Listening, and Request to Modify and coach the participants in how they will use them.

C. Gain commitment from each that if they plan to offer a Full Apology during the joint session, that they will offer them sincerely. And if an apology is offered, they will accept it graciously, if possible. If they cannot accept the apology, they cannot summarily reject it. They simply need to say, "Thank you for the apology."

D. Identify what, exactly, each person will change in their behavior.

E. Gain a commitment from each that, during the joint session, they will clearly communicate these changes and formally commit to making them.

F. Gain commitment from each that once the other person honors their commitment and starts to make the changes they committed to, they will make a good faith effort to let go of resentments and work productively together.

Time It Takes: *30-45 minutes per participant*

Restoring Respect

Overview. This step also usually occurs during session five, after you've determined what the participants want and need from each other so that they can move forward and work together productively and effectively without the tension generated by the "what happened."

In this part of the session, you'll be reminding them again of the *"It-Takes-Two-To-Tango"* concept and that if they truly want to work together, then both the Aggrieved and the Accused must commit to doing things differently.

Generally, both must commit to changing behaviors that the other person feels are *disrespectful* and to engage in behaviors that the other feels are *respectful*.

They must commit that if they offer a "Full Apology," it must be done sincerely. If they are the recipient of an apology, they must commit to accepting graciously, or at least not reject it out of hand.

Additionally, both must commit to being willing to make a good faith effort to re-establish the working relationship once these changes are made. And it's possible you'll be coaching them on letting go of some of their anger, upset, and resentment related to the "what happened."

Now, at first, the Aggrieved may say, "Hey, they disrespected me, why do I need to change?"

You've got at least two responses:

Words You Can Use.

1. "As you may recall, earlier in the process you admitted to engaging in disrespectful behavior yourself during or after the initial "what happened." You'll need to commit to owning your behavior to the other person when we come together in the joint session, to apologizing for it, and to how you're going to behave differently going forward."

2. "I realize that you feel that you didn't do anything wrong. But remember, in Step Seven you identified that you wanted a Full Apology from the Accused. You're going to have to make a commitment now as to how you're going to respond if they do make that Full Apology. And saying, 'we'll see how they do with their apology,' isn't enough. If you want a Full Apology and they make it sincerely, then they're going to expect that you'll accept their apology. Are you prepared to do that? They're also going to expect a commitment from you on the behaviors that you're going to engage in that will enable the working relationship to function effectively and productively going forward."

Step Eight

As for the Accused, we've found that by this point in the process, many are aware that their behavior was considered disrespectful, are willing to own it and make a "Full Apology."

However, it's possible that defensiveness may raise its ugly head once again and the Accused may try to justify, excuse, or minimize their behavior. This is common and you can allow it for a short time. Some people just need to "vent" to get their excuses off their chest and feel heard before they can start working on owning and then letting go of that behavior. You'll want to use "Reflective Listening" (see later this section) to help them feel heard being careful never to approve nor agree with their justifications and excuses.

Eventually, you'll need to remind them that people feel what they feel and it's not our place to tell them how they should react to what we say and do. If we want to have a working relationship with someone, then we must own our behaviors, regardless of why, and the negative impacts they had. You may need to come back to this point several times during this step and again during the joint session in Step Nine.

The "Full Apology." We developed the Full Apology after watching public figures, politicians, and business leaders repeatedly make half-hearted or non-apology-apologies that fell flat or backfired. Many of these incorporated what we call "weasel words," such as "I'm sorry *if* you were offended," and "I'm sorry *you thought* what I said was disrespectful," and "I'm sorry *some* people were offended, *but it was because....*"

A sincere Full Apology never equivocates, never makes excuses, and never accuses someone else of being too sensitive.

Here are the *Seven Steps of a Full Apology:*

1. **Admit it.** Admit, specifically, what you did/said and that you know it was disrespectful. This is often called "owning it."

2. **Describe How It Hurt Them.** They need to know that you know how and why they felt disrespected.

3. **Make No Excuses.** Saying, "I'm sorry, but . . . " or, "I did it because . . . " are excuses. Simply say, "There are no excuses," or "I have no excuse."

4. **Apologize Sincerely and Ask for Forgiveness.** Usually, people who feel disrespected want to hear a sincere "I'm sorry." And, by asking

for forgiveness, you're putting yourself in a vulnerable position to be rejected or disrespected by them, which switches the power dynamic considerably and can make a significant, positive difference going forward.

5. **Promise: Never Again.** If you're truly sorry, and you're a responsible person, then you will not behave disrespectfully again. Some people don't like to say this; they're afraid of being boxed into a corner. But, if you do behave disrespectfully again, then the chances of your apology being accepted, and respect being restored are close to nil.

6. **Offer to Make Amends.** By doing this, you're indicating that you sincerely want to make things right, that you're not going to just apologize and forget about what happened. Even if they don't need or want you to make amends, the offer is important.

7. **Start Immediately.** Start making amends, start behaving respectfully immediately, and keep it up. A Full Apology is just the start to repairing a relationship, and actions speak louder than words.

As the coach of the *CfR* process, you can rest assured that you will be helping one or both participants to formulate a Full Apology at some point. In fact, you may be helping some of the bystanders and other stakeholders develop "Full Apologies" too.

Reflective Listening. During the joint session in Step Nine, the participants will be talking with each other and expressing their feelings. Both parties need to feel "heard." To facilitate this, you'll use a technique called "Reflective Listening." It's a very simple, yet highly effective tool for ensuring people with strong feelings feel that they are being heard by the person who they believe disrespected them. It's very likely you're familiar with it and used it yourself. Here's how it goes:

● Person A states their feelings.

● Person B says Person A's name, followed by "What I think I'm hearing you say is . . . ," and then uses Person A's words to paraphrase the *essence* of what was said back to them.

● When Person B is done paraphrasing, they'll ask, "Have I got that right?"

Step Eight

- Person A will either confirm that Person B got it right, or say, "Not quite, what I'm saying is . . . ," and then rephrase it while striving for clarity.

- Person B will listen, and when Person A is done, say, "OK, what I think I'm hearing you say is . . . ," and again paraphrase for the *essence,* and then ask, "Now have I got that right?"

Since you'll be facilitating the use of Reflective Listening repeatedly during step nine, you need to introduce it to the participants here in Step Eight, telling them that this is something they'll be using frequently during the next step.

Developing a Change List. Also in Step Eight, you're going to coach each person to make a list of behaviors that they're going to change including what they're going to *stop* saying and doing and what they're going to *start* saying and doing. This must include, at the very least, a commitment to never again engage in the behavior that was involved in the "what happened" and was perceived to be disrespectful.

One of the easiest ways to elicit ideas about what they will commit to doing is to say:

Words You Can Use.

"By now we have a good sense of what you consider to be disrespectful and respectful. Now, I want you to put yourself in the other person's shoes and imagine how they want to be treated by you. What do you think they feel is respectful?"

This list should include specific behaviors. Essentially, you're trying to help this person determine how they're going to interact with the other person while bearing in mind the *Platinum Rule: Do unto others as they want to be done unto.*

If your participant is having trouble coming up with ideas, you may have to take off your coaching cap and put on your consulting cap, advising each participant on what behaviors may be appropriate. You could say:

"I wonder if this might be an idea, XYZ?"

Restoring Respect

Whatever language and behaviors make it onto the list, the participants must be willing to articulate them clearly during Step Nine.

Request to Modify. Toward the end of this step, you're going to introduce a technique called "Request to Modify." Essentially, during the joint session, while they are sharing their Change Lists with each other, one or both may be dissatisfied with what is being proposed by the other because it doesn't meet their needs or wants. If this happens, they can make a "Request to Modify," where they will articulate clearly what they want modified and why. The other person may choose to agree to the request or not and you'll assist with facilitating this discussion. But once the request has either been granted or denied, that's the end of it, and they must move on. Either participant can make a Request to Modify during the process.

Step Eight Worksheet

Here's a worksheet for notating behaviors:

A. Past Behavior: _____
_____

B. Changes to:_____
_____

A. Past Behavior: _____
_____

B. Changes to:_____
_____

A. Past Behavior: _____
_____

B. Changes to:_____
_____

A. Past Behavior: _____
_____

B. Changes to:_____
_____

A. Past Behavior: _____
_____

B. Changes to:_____
_____

You cannot shake hands with a clenched fist.
—Indira Gandhi

Coaching for Respect™
Step Nine

Facilitating the Joint Coaching Session

Goals for Step Nine:

A. Bring the participants together in person for a joint session in a private, neutral location that's comfortable, quiet, and relatively informal.

B. Ensure they understand what this session is designed to do: to name what they genuinely respect in each other, jointly agree on the facts of the "what happened," express feelings in a way that each feels "heard," offer apologies as appropriate, and create a mutually agreed upon plan for the language and behaviors they're going to let go of and take on moving forward.

C. Ensure you review the "what happened"—without adding your own spin and/or interpretations of their feelings and reactions—to the point where both agree that the facts, language, and behaviors, etc. occurred as described.

D. Ensure the participants bear in mind some of the important concepts around respect and disrespect they've been hearing from you all along.

E. Ensure they express their feelings responsibly and respectfully and use Reflective Listening to ensure each feels "heard."

F. Ensure that if Full Apologies are offered, that they are offered sincerely following the model they've been given and that the recipient accepts them graciously or at least does not reject them out of hand.

G. Ensure the participants express their Wants and Needs that they want met by the other going forward.

H. Ensure that the participants agree and delineate verbally and in writing on the language and behaviors they are committed to engaging in going forward. Get them to sign the agreement.

Time It Takes: *Varies, from 1-3 hours*

Overview. Finally, you've reached the joint session. This is where you bring the participants together to help bring closure to the "what happened," ensure everyone feels "heard," facilitate apologies, and to support them in designing and committing to a way of working together going forward. Interestingly, this session can go quite easily and smoothly if you've been thorough in completing the goals of each of the previous steps and both participants are acting in full integrity.

There is a kind of art and process to this step which is different from the others. As follows:

Room Set Up: Very often the participants come into this session assuming they are going to sit across a conference table from each other, with you at the head, mediating between them. But that's too formal and sends the message that this session is adversarial. That's the last thing you want.

Instead, you should choose a space with three comfortable sitting chairs set near to and gently facing one another so that no one is forced to strain their neck to make eye contact or speak loudly to be heard. Make sure that there is no table between the chairs, except perhaps a low coffee table for water and snacks. Avoid harsh lighting and loud, intrusive music or noise. It should be private, with little chance of interruption. Also, if possible, you'll want to identify another room, space, or place very close by where you can conduct a private **"Sidebar"** discussion with one or the other if needed *(see below)*.

You'll want to have water, coffee, other beverages and perhaps a few sweets available (cookies and chocolate seem to make all meetings better). Keep a box of tissues nearby, but out of sight, just in case there are tears (not uncommon!). In short, the space you're using for this joint session should help the participants feel as relaxed and as comfortable as it's possible to be in this situation.

Lastly, you should provide notepads and pens to the participants which they'll be using throughout. And you'll need a laptop and access to a printer so that you can draw up their final Agreement, print out three copies and have them sign them in front of each other. If you don't have these tools, be aware that you will need to draw up the agreement by hand.

The Joint Session Script. This joint session flows through seven distinct, consecutive phases. It's imperative that, more than any other step in the *CfR* process, you move through these phases one by one and very deliberately. We've given you a script that you can use which you'll find at the end of this section. But, we can't emphasize this enough: *do not "wing" Step Nine, follow the script very closely.* You don't have to memorize the script, but you should become very, very familiar with it. Winging it just won't work and could end up making everything worse.

Ground Rules. Although it might go easy and well, this session can also be intense for all. You'll need to set some ground rules, as follows:

A. Your phones should be set to silent and put away. If you need them to refer to your notes, then they need to be set on Airplane Mode.

B. We'll take a break or breaks as needed just to use the facilities and breathe for moment.

C. Do your utmost to be decent, respectful, and civil to each other. No raising of voices or disrespectful language or behavior.

D. Use Reflective Listening throughout and listen to understand, not to respond.

E. If you have questions about the process as we go through it, just ask me.

Your Facilitator's Cap is On: During all of the previous steps you've been wearing your coach's cap, working alone with one participant at a time, and doing all of the things a coach does. But, in Step Nine, you're wearing a different cap, Facilitator. You should make this distinction right at the beginning and remind them that you're facilitating during this session, not coaching.

Restoring Respect

We. Both. Together. In general, you must talk in this session as if everyone is in this together. Use words and phrases like, "we," "both," "both of you," "the three of us," and "together" frequently to imply that this is a collaboration, a team effort. In fact, it's helpful to use words like "collaboration," "cooperation," and "mutually helpful," throughout.

Do your utmost to stay positive and enthusiastic, complimenting them when they say something respectfully and thoughtfully. If they seem emotional, encourage them to take their time and a breath before speaking, or to rephrase if they believe they've said something awkwardly.

You should also acknowledge the difficulty of what they're trying to do together and tell them how much you appreciate the time and effort they've both put in to get to this step in the process.

Follow The Process. You'll need to follow the process outlined below, doing your utmost to stick to the script as we've advised, driving forward gently, but firmly to the end state where you have agreement and a commitment from both on how they are going to interact respectfully going forward. It rolls out in seven phases:

1) *What Is Respected:* You will begin by prompting the Aggrieved to talk about one thing they respect in the Accused. The Accused will use Reflective Listening and then talk about one thing they respect in the Aggrieved and the Aggrieved will use Reflective Listening, and so on, back and forth, until the lists are complete.

2) *The Facts of the "What Happened."* You'll lay out the facts of the "what happened," without your own spin or descriptions of how people reacted and get agreement from both on the facts.

3) *Reactions.* You'll prompt each person to talk about how they reacted and were impacted, including how they felt. Throughout this phase, you'll ask the other person to use Reflective Listening so that both feel heard by the other.

4) *Apologies.* You'll prompt one or both to offer a Full Apology and have the recipient of the apology use Reflective Listening.

5) *Wants and Needs.* You'll prompt both to summarize their wants and needs that they would like to be met so that they feel comfortable going forward.

6) *Change Lists.* You'll prompt both to go over their Change Lists with each other, specifically detailing what behaviors and language is going to change and how. You'll allow them to make "Requests to Modify" from each other which are often based on their Wants and Needs. After discussion and consideration, the person being asked to modify the behavior they planned to start using will decide if they will accept or reject the request.

7) *Final Commitments.* After writing down and printing out their commitments to each other, you'll prompt them to review them with each other, make final modifications, verbally commit to them, and then formally commit to them in writing with their signatures. Each will receive a signed copy of the agreement. You'll schedule the first round of check-in calls at this time and remind them about confidentiality.

Why Start With Respect? You'll notice the process begins with the participants telling each other the specific things they respect in them. This is very deliberate and is based on the Neuroscience of Respect. When you tell someone that you genuinely respect them and specifically what it is you respect in them, they perceive this as kind. They feel "good," they feel complimented, more confident and prepared to discuss difficult issues. Research consistently shows that people who feel genuinely respected are more likely to be open to discussing their behaviors and communication styles that are considered to be problematic. So, by leading off with what they respect in each other, you're putting the participants in a much better frame of mind and positioning the joint session for success.

Sidebar. It's possible that one or the other may start to waver or become hesitant during this session. Perhaps they've heard something that's triggered some emotional memories and they become overwhelmed. Or they may come to feel that the other person is being particularly insensitive, insincere, or "out of integrity." Or, once they get into a conversation about the "what happened," they decide that they don't want to work with this person after all. These are real possibilities that you'll need to be aware of and prepare for.

This is where a Sidebar (a private discussion with one of the participants), can be particularly useful. Typically, you'll sense someone is starting to waver or become anxious before they say anything about it. You may hear them say,

"I'm not sure this is a good idea," or, "Now that I'm here with them, I don't think I can do this."

Don't panic! Simply take a deep breath and ask them to step away with you for a Sidebar. Usually, they're relieved that you suggested it.

The Sidebar is the one time during Step Nine that you'll need to put your coaching cap back on. Often as not, they're nervous about whether this joint session is really going to result in the other person changing their behavior. Your goal is to de-escalate their upset, remind them of their commitment to follow through and the time and effort they've put in, and their goal of completing the process.

Here's how you conduct a Sidebar. Once you've taken them out of view and earshot of the other person, avoid starting the Sidebar by asking, "What's up?" Instead, start by saying, "Here's what I'm noticing." Then, describe the signs of anxiety, tension, reluctance that you're sensing and make an educated guess as to why you think they're feeling these things. Since you've been coaching both participants in private, you'll probably have a good idea of what's driving these feelings and you should say so. Confirm that you're on target.

If you are, then you should remind them about the Neuroscience of Respect, the commitments they made, and the fact that they've come this far and have committed to seeing it through.

If you're not on target, they'll tell you that they have other concerns, and you'll need to address those concerns or promise to address them when you go back into the joint session.

Note: there have been two times in my career where something was revealed in a Sidebar that forced me to shut down the joint session completely. In one case someone realizing during the joint session that they couldn't commit to going forward with a working relationship with the other person. In the other case, I found out new information that made it clear that one of the participants was out of integrity. Both times it was disappointing to shut the process down, but it had to be done.

One last point before we dive into the script for the joint session: defensiveness. It's very likely that one or both participants are going to start defending themselves, or at least they'll take up time trying to explain or make excuses for their behavior. *Do not let them do it.* The time for making excuses and defending oneself is long gone. This session is all about them owning their behavior, apologizing for it (if appropriate), and working with the other person to create a plan to move forward.

Step Nine Process Script. Words You Can Use

Note: for the purposes of this script, the actual words you should say are in a

sans serif typeface without italics with a gray background.

The instructions you should follow are in a serif font in italics. We've named the Aggrieved "GG," and the Accused "CC." The lines below each item are for your notes.

1. Arrive/Set Up.

You arrive first and set up the space so that it's comfortable. Ensure the participants are NOT sitting at a table across from each other.

_____

2. Welcome.

Welcome them as they arrive and seat them comfortably. Give them note pads and pens, make sure they turn off their phones and have easy access to the beverages and any food that's available.

_____

_____

3. Thank You.

Thank you for being here. I really appreciate you both taking the time and putting in all the effort to get us to this place. I want to acknowledge that what we've been doing over these weeks hasn't been easy and you're both to be commended for sticking with it and getting us to this point.

_____

_____

4. Facilitator's Cap.

In our previous sessions, I was wearing my coaching cap. Today I'm wearing my facilitator's cap. My role is to support you both in bringing this process to a successful conclusion. This means I'll be reminding you to use the techniques you learned during coaching, sometimes repeatedly. Also, I want to remind you about confidentiality: what's said in here, stays in here.

_____

_____

5. Agenda/Goals.

Here's our agenda and goals for today. We're going to . . .

a. Talk about what we respect in the other person. Then, we'll . . .

b. Review the 'what happened' to make sure there's agreement on the facts. After this, we'll . . .

c. Review and relate the feelings that were generated by the 'what happened' so that each of you can feel 'heard' by the other. Then, you will . . .

d. Offer and receive apologies as appropriate. Then, we'll . . .

e. Take a quick break.

f. After the break, you'll describe your Wants and Needs in order to feel comfortable going forward with the relationship. Then, you'll . . .

g. Together, develop lists of language and behaviors that you're both committed to letting go of and engaging in going forward. You'll work together on these, modify as needed, agree to them verbally and then in writing.

h. Our overall goal for today is the same as it's been throughout the entire process: for you both to feel comfortable enough with the relationship so that you can work together productively and effectively.

_____

_____

6. Techniques We're Using.

A few words about the techniques we'll be using today, all of which I've mentioned and practiced with you in previous sessions.

_____

_____

7. Reflective Listening.

We'll be using Reflective Listening, where one of you makes a statement and then the other reflects it back by saying, '(Name) I think I'm hearing you say XYZ,' then you paraphrase what they said using their words, followed by, 'Have I got that right?' We'll be using Reflective Listening throughout this meeting. It may feel a bit awkward and tedious, but I need to insist that we do it because it's so effective in helping each of you to feel heard.

_____

_____

8. Emotions/Upset.

Whenever I sense that you're feeling emotional or upset, I will ask you to take a deep breath, and then to take your time before you speak. I'll ask you to speak thoughtfully about your emotions, trying your utmost to express yourself authentically while taking care to avoid saying things in a way that increases the tension.

_____

_____

9. Apologies.

One or both of you may be making a Full Apology today. Doing this requires courage and sincerity. Receiving a Full Apology also requires courage and compassion as well. I want to acknowledge and commend both of you for being willing to do these things.

_____

_____

10. Sidebar.

If you need to have a Sidebar conversation with me, we'll do that. I may also call for a Sidebar myself if it seems to me that we're stuck, or something needs to be addressed individually.

_____

_____

11. Ground Rules.

Lastly, here are the ground rules for this session.

☐ Your phones should be set to silent and put away. If you need them to refer to your notes, then they need to be set on Airplane Mode.

☐ We'll take a break or breaks as needed just to use the facilities and breathe for moment.

☐ Do your utmost to be decent, respectful, and civil to each other. No raising of voices or disrespectful language or behavior.

☐ Use Reflective Listening throughout and listen to understand, not to respond.

☐ If you have questions about the process as we go through it, just ask me.

_____

_____

Okay, let's start.

12. Phase One: Respect.

This is Phase One. You'll recall that I coached you on identifying the things you respected about the other person. I'm going to ask GG (use aggreved's name) to start by telling CC (use asccused's name) one thing you respect about them. Then CC will use Reflective Listening. Then we'll switch and CC will tell GG one thing they respect in them, and GG will use Reflective Listening. We'll go back and forth until your lists are done. By the way, I've always found that during this part of the process, some people are surprised to hear what the other person respects in them. They didn't know it. That's great. Just go with it and accept it.

GG, I'd like you to start. What's one thing you respect in CC?

GG tells one thing they respect in CC; CC uses Reflective Listening. You'll work back and forth with them until both have told each other what they respect in each other.

_____

_____

13. Phase Two: Review the Facts of the "What Happened."

Okay, now we're moving into Phase Two. I'm going to describe the 'what happened' as I understand it and ensure that both of you agree on it. Here are the facts as I understand them."

Describe the "what happened" briefly and succinctly, taking care to avoid using 'judging' language or mentioning the feelings the participants had at the time that they shared with you. When you're done say,

I'd like to hear from you both, have I described the facts of the 'what happened' accurately?

Usually, they will say yes. If they don't, ask them,

What facts have I missed? Just the facts.

Work toward common agreement.

_____

_____

14. Phase Three: Reactions.

Okay now we're moving onto Phase Three which focuses on your reactions to the 'what happened.' I'm going to ask GG will talk about the reactions and feelings they had during and after the 'what happened.' From time to time, as GG is doing this, I'm going to ask CC to use Reflective Listening to ensure that GG feels heard by CC.

Also, after GG has their turn, CC may want to express their feelings that came up during the 'what happened,' and in that case, GG will use Reflective Listening as well.

Neither of you is going to be permitted to defend yourself to the other. If you try, I'll ask you to stop, respectfully of course.

GG describes their feelings; CC uses Reflective Listening. You'll stay with GG expressing their feelings, and CC reflecting them back until GG is done and it's clear that they felt heard.

_____

_____

15. Accused's Reaction.

Next, CC is going to talk about reactions and feelings they may have had during and after the 'what happened.' Again, I may ask GG to use Reflective Listening from time to time. Please remember, feelings are feelings, we all have them.

CC describes their feelings; GG uses Reflective Listening. You'll stay with CC expressing their feelings, and GG reflecting them back until CC is done and it's clear that they felt heard.

_____

_____

16. Phase Four: Full Apologies.

Okay, now we're moving onto Phase Four.

Here you turn to the person who has already committed to making a "Full Apology." Note: if both are planning to apologize, you'll have to determine who should go first. Typically, the Accused should go first because assuming they apologize sincerely and effectively, it may be easier for the Aggrieved to make their own apology.

Okay CC, you committed to me that you would offer a Full Apology, please go ahead.

The apology is offered.

Okay GG, please use Reflective Listening to reflect what CC said.

GG does this.

GG, now that you've reflected what CC said, is there anything you'd like to say to them? Please remain respectful.
Okay now CC please use Reflective Listening to describe what you heard GG say.

And so on until the apologies are made and either accepted or not rejected out of hand and they've simply said, 'Thank you for your apology.'

_____

_____

BREAK.

We'll take a very quick break now to use the facilities, go outside and breathe. and come back together in 5 minutes. Please don't get on your phones or respond to messages. We don't have time for that, and I need you to stay focused on what we're doing.

Unless they've been moving fast, you should take a break here. Everyone will need a breather.

_____

_____

17. Phase Five: Wants and Needs.

Okay, we're now moving onto Phase Five. When we started this process, you told me about things you wanted and needed from the other person in order for you to feel comfortable going forward with this relationship. We're going to go through those now, and we'll use Reflective Listening on each item. I'll also ask you to make notes during this phase because when we start talking about the things you're going to change, you may want to modify them based on the other person's Wants and Needs. GG, I'd like you to start. What is one of your wants and need from CC?"

Go back and forth between them until all their Wants and Needs have been expressed.

_____

_____

18. Phase Six: Change Lists.

Okay, we're moving onto Phase Six. Now is the time for you to pull out your 'Change Lists.' We're going to start with CC talking about a past behavior and how that's going to change. But before we do, please remember that if you feel that you want to modify what the other proposes to change, then you can make a 'Request to Modify' and we'll discuss it. *(See Step Eight.)* Okay CC, what's the past behavior at the top of your list and how is that going to change?

CC offers their first change.

Okay GG, use Reflective Listening to paraphrase back what is it you heard that CC is going to change and how.

GG does so.

Okay GG, are you good with that change?

Assuming they say "yes," then say . . .

Okay GG, now it's your turn, what is the past behavior at the top of your list and how is that going to change?

GG offers their first change and CC will use Reflective Listening, offer their acceptance of it and so on until the lists are complete. You have been making notes of their commitments throughout this section.

Print out three copies, one for each participant and one for you as a reference for when you conduct your check-in calls with them.

_____

_____

19. Phase Seven: Final Commitments.

Okay, we're now in Phase Seven, which is the final phase today. You've both told each other what you're going to change going forward and you've agreed to these with modifications. I've them written down here in this Agreement. Let's review them to see if I've captured it all correctly. After I read each one, I'll check with you both to see if you agree.

Read through each out loud, check for accuracy, and check for agreement after each one. Once you've revised them, print out three copies.

Now, I'd like you both to commit verbally to each other to doing what you said you are going to do. You're going to shake hands while you say this to each other, "I'm committed to doing what I've said I'll do." CC, you're first.

Okay now that you've committed verbally, you're going to sign all three copies of this Agreement and then shake hands again.

Both commit verbally, shake hands, then sign all three copies of the Agreement and shake hands. Note: you do not sign the Agreement, this is between them.

GG and CC, we're done with Phase Seven. Well done, both of you.

---

20. Next Steps.

Okay, here's what happens next. I'm going to report to the stakeholders that the process is complete, that the Agreement has been signed and that they should expect that you both will honor your commitments. I'm not sharing this Agreement with them; this is between the two of you. But they will also expect that you will start working together more productively and effectively going forward.

Also, I'm going to be checking in with each of you a couple of times in the next month or so to see how it's going. I'll have my copy of this Agreement in front of me. If it looks like past behaviors are cropping up again, then we'll have to come together and work all through this again. I have a hunch you'd both rather not do that.

Get out your calendars and let's schedule the first check-in calls now.

Again, what was said and agreed to in here stays in here.

Okay then, thank you both! We're done and don't forget to take your copy of the Agreement with you. Please keep it secure.

If you need to, make some final notes to yourself about how it went and what you can expect going forward and then gather up your materials, and clean up the room. I urge you not to go back to work. Instead, go home, and take a break. You've earned it.

I've learned that people will forget what you said,
people will forget what you did, but people
will never forget how you made them feel.
—Maya Angelou

Coaching for Respect™
Step Ten

Reporting in/Following Up

Step Ten Goals:

A. Report into the Stakeholders (HR, Legal, Leadership) either verbally or in writing that the process has been completed, or not. Advise them that the participants have made commitments to each other which they have agreed to honor. Do *not* share the written Agreement.

B. Advise Stakeholders that you will be checking in with both participants at least twice in the next two to eight weeks to determine if the commitments are being honored and assess the state of the relationship.

C. Advise Stakeholders that it's possible that you will not be needed any more, or that you may need to individually coach the participants more and/or bring them back into another joint session, TBD.

D. Check in with each participant, with the Agreement in front of you, at least twice during the next two to eight weeks.

Time It Takes: *varies (depending on how many), 10-30 minutes to report into the Stakeholders verbally; 15-45 minutes per participant per check-in.*

Restoring Respect

Overview. Although you're not going to provide details or the Agreement, it's your responsibility to report into the Stakeholders that the process is complete, or not. Usually, there's no need to do this in person. You can do this verbally over the phone or in a videocall. You should simply advise them the process is complete. If asked, you can give them your sense of how it went and your level of confidence that the relationship is on its way to being repaired to the point where the participants can work together comfortably enough to be productive and effective. But you don't have to if you'd rather not. It's your decision.

During this call, you'll also remind the Stakeholders that you'll be checking in with each of the participants at least twice in the next three to eight weeks and that you keep them up to speed on progress or if you need to do any additional coaching.

If the process is *not* completed because you shut it down or one of the participants pulled out, you'll need to inform the Stakeholders at the time the process stopped. Again, you shouldn't provide details as to why the process stopped other than it did stop and was not completed. Remind them that this was a possibility and refer them to your contract if they insist on details. If you're asked if you think the relationship was repaired, you can give your informed assessment if you'd like, or simply say, "I don't know."

As for the participant Check-Ins, a phone call or videocall will work for these as well. You'll want to make both calls on the same day and have a copy of the Agreement in front of you when you do.

Check-In Calls. Your first check-in call should be approximately two weeks after the joint session. You should have scheduled it with the participants during the joint session. Your second call should come about four to six weeks after the first.

You can start by asking, "How's it going so far?" It's likely they'll respond with "fine," or "not so good."

If they say "fine," and you can tell they mean it, that's great. But "fine" can have many meanings including, "not so good." So, listen carefully to their tone. No matter how they respond, you should then dive into the Agreement and go through the items one by one with them. If there's a problem, it will be surfaced.

If All Is Well. If you sense that all is going as planned and people are honoring the Agreement and their commitments, then after you've gone through it thoroughly, tell them you're happy for them, that it appears that everything is going as planned, and that you'll check in again in a few weeks. Hopefully, both participants will report that all is well during both of your calls. That's the ideal outcome.

If It's Not So Good. We're all human beings and changing habits are tough. So, it's entirely possible that one or both of your participants may respond that things aren't going so well because someone isn't honoring the Agreement or has fallen out of integrity on their commitments, or some other behavior has cropped up that's negatively impacting the relationship. You'll need to do some digging, fact-finding, and coaching to determine the severity of the problem.

For example, are they being hyper-vigilant or hyper-sensitive to the new reality of the relationship and need some coaching on being patient and/or tolerant? Or are they once again feeling so disrespected that they're thinking they don't want to work with the other person anymore? If that's the case, then you'll need to press hard: are they sure they're done trying to make this work? If they are, what do they want to do? Then, you may have to coach them on next steps. If they say that they're going to quit, then you can coach them during this call on how they're going to do that if they ask for coaching. But since you're technically under contract with their organization, that's as far as you can take it.

By the way, even though you are professionally obligated to inform the Stakeholders if a participant is planning to take an action that may have an immediate and significantly negative impact on persons or the organization—such as theft or threats of violence, etc.—you are not obligated to inform Stakeholders that someone intends to quit. That is the participant's job. You are permitted to coach them on how to do that ethically and responsibly.

You should know that it's never your role to inform the Stakeholders that one or both participants is unable or unwilling to go forward working with the other person. That's the participants' job. But, during your check-in you can coach them on how they're going to do that, or what their other options might be. Usually, that will be the last coaching session you'll have with them.

*Those people who develop the ability to continuously acquire
new and better forms of knowledge that they can apply to their
work and to their lives will be the movers and shakers in our
society for the indefinite future.*

—Brian Tracy

Section V ■
Final Thoughts . . .
Invitation to Become Certified

When I think about trying to help people learn about respect and to be more respectful, civil, kind and compassionate to each other, I'm more than willing to admit that it isn't easy. In fact, the first time I ran the *CfR* process many years ago, I was a nervous wreck, certain that it was going to blow up in my face. But I was fortunate, I had two decent people to work with who really wanted to restore respect to their work relationship. Their apologies were sincere and heartfelt, and expressing respect for each other made all the difference. That time, the process worked as planned.

But there have been other times where the process didn't work at all and I had to assess where I might have played a role in it's failure, and reassure myself that no matter what, I did the best I could.

So let's face it, learning about and running the *CfR* process is a significant investment of your time and energy. It's not for everyone. But if it's something you feel called to do, then I strongly urge you to make another important and worthy investment—become certified in *CfR*.

At the Center for Respectful Leadership we have developed a *CfR* Certification program that is uniquely powerful and effective. Not only is it designed and led by me and other certified, expert instructors, it also makes use of the training techniques we are famous for, including experiential learning, live, professional theater and improvisation, and customized "living case studies" based on the kinds of situations and employees that you tell us you're dealing with.

Program Features. Our *CfR* Certification program has the following features:

- Small class size—comprised of dedicated professionals like you.

- Expert, *CfR* Certified Instructors.

- Three Days in a comfortable, safe, professional yet relaxed, fully equipped learning environment.

- Performances of "living case studies" by, and guided improvisation sessions with professional actors who walk and talk like real employees in your organization and who are also very familiar with the *CfR* process.

- Participant Guides, Job Aides, and *CfR* resources such as workbooks and templates.

- Multiple opportunities for you to practice your new skills in small, supportive groups and receive expert feedback.

- Post-Program individual coaching and consulting sessions with the instructors.

- Access to all of the Center for Respectful Leadership's resources, videos, and guides for free or discounted prices.

- Referrals to clients who are seeking *CfR* Coach/Facilitators.

Key Learnings. In the *CfR* Certification Program, you will learn:

- ✓ How to run the *CfR* process effectively and efficiently.

- ✓ How to explain the process to Stakeholders and Participants.

- ✓ Why respect and disrespect play significant roles in business outcomes.

- ✓ How to coach participants in preparation for the joint session.

- ✓ How to manage defensiveness, upset, and pushback effectively.

- ✓ How to successfully facilitate the joint session.

Final Thoughts

✓ How to contract to facilitate the *CfR* process as an external provider.

✓ How to leverage the Center for Respectful Leadership's extensive resources to your and your client's benefit.

Please join us in one of our *CfR* Certification programs. It will be one of the best investments in your professional development that you'll ever make.

The first responsibility of a leader is to define reality.
The last is to say thank you.
—Max de Pree

Section VI ■
Acknowledgements

Anyone who's written a book knows that it takes a village, as they say. This one certainly did. Here are my thanks to all of the villagers who helped me with *Restoring Respect.*

First, I thank my dear colleague and friend, Cindy Burnham who not only served as an incredible proofreader, but also as a content editor and commentator providing extremely valuable insight and expertise before and during the writing of *Restoring Respect.* She's a highly experienced expert in running the *CfR* process, and a tremendous resource and executive coach. Thank you, Cindy!

Secondly, I thank Marshall Goldsmith and his colleague Kate Clark at Marshall Goldsmith, Inc. for agreeing to craft the fabulous foreword to *Restoring Respect.* It's truly an honor to have our work supported and championed by Marshall and his colleagues.

I also thank the many wonderful colleagues who took a look at the drafts of *Restoring Respect* and gave me their feedback, recommendations and testimonials, including Adam Noakes, Gerald Finch, Jordan Goldrich, Maya Hu-Chan, Paul Nichols, and Sarah Chapman Bacerra, the Center for Respectful Leadership's Chief Learning Officer.

And thank you to all the good people—many of whom are clients as well as colleagues and friends—who provided me with a quote for the back cover or inside front pages, including Ana Melikian, CB Bowman, Catherine Mattice,

Restoring Respect

Cellene Hoogenkamp, Eddie Turner, Frank Wagner, Jon Saunders, Mark Snow, Morag Barrett, Rachel Soloff, Sally Helgesen, and Tom Deverell, the Executive Vice President of CRL's Executive Coaching Forums.

A shout out to all the folks who gave me their thoughts on the book title, including Bill Guyan, Karen Helmacy, Joslyn Barroso, Nicole Whalen, and Tracie Cruse at Leonardo DRS, Elika Dadsetan-Foley, Denise Kulesa, Jan Thompson, Kevin Rafferty, LaPonda Fitchpatrick, Maresa Friedman, Mark Schall, Patti Perez, Raydiance Dangerfield, Robert Makar, and the brilliant Chris Witt, who came up with the final version.

A big "thank you for your patience and creativity" goes to David Maxine, cover and book designer extraordinaire, and to Walter G. Meyer, my co-author of *The Respectful Leader* and an expert who knows the book writing and publishing world like nobody else, and who has a sense of humor . . . like nobody else.

Also, I thank the staff of the Center for Respectful Leadership including our Operations Manager Amy Jo Davies, Angie Schultz our Director of Design and User Experience, and Katilyn Standlee our Director of Outreach. Amy Jo, you've been particularly helpful in taking on so many of the tasks I should have been doing instead of writing this book. I can't thank you enough.

A special thanks to all of our many clients all over the world—especially those in leadership and human resources—who continue to believe in me and the work of the Center for Respectful Leadership. It is truly an honor to be of service to you and your organizations. Thank you!

Lastly, I want to thank my life partner Kathleen Aaron, who kept encouraging me to keep going, who picked me up when I was doubting myself, and who gives me unconditional love every single day. You're the best and I love you.

—Gregg Ward

PS—If your name was mistakenly ommitted from this list of villagers, I sincerely apologize and thank you as an unsung hero to me and our work at the Center for Respectful Leadership.

Words matter, and the right words matter most of all.
In the end they're all that remain of us.
—John Birmingham

Section VII ◼
Glossary of Terms

Accused. A person who's been accused of behaving disrespectfully; called "CC" in the script used during the joint session, Step Nine. The Accused can also be aggrieved by others' disrespect.

Aggrieved. A person who feels disrespected; called "GG" in the script that is used during the joint session, Step Nine. The Aggrieved can also be accused of disrespect.

Amygdala Hijack. A physiological response to a threat, including disrespect, in which the person who feels disrespected goes into "fight, flight, or freeze" mode as a result of hormones being released into the body, and is temporarily unable to think rationally or thoughtfully.

Bystanders. Others who heard, saw, or were negatively impacted by others' disrespectful language and behaviors.

Carrott and Stick Leadership. A traditional leadership style. In essence it means, "If you do as I say and achieve the goal, you'll be rewarded. But if you don't, you'll be punished." Although effective in commission-based sales environments, today many consider it to be too simplistic and disrespectful.

Coaching for Respect™ **process.** A ten step coaching and facilitation process, developed by Gregg Ward of the Center for Respectful Leadership, that is used to restore respect to a work relationship after respect has been lost. Typically, the initial coaching and facilitation rolls out over the course of six to eight weeks.

Coaching Cap. A metaphorical cap, or hat, worn while coaching someone and when using the techniques of coaching such as asking questions, challenging assumptions, etc. Typically, you might say, "I'm putting on my Coaching Cap now."

Command and Control Leadership. A traditional leadership style. In essence it means, "Do as I say because I'm the boss." This is a classic leadership style which is often used in the military and para-military organizations. It can be very effective when lives are at stake, but when they are not, many of today's workers find it disrespectful.

Confirmation Bias. In the context of respect in relationships, confirmation bias means that after someone has felt disrespected, they are more likely to view the person who disrespected them through a negative lens. People are often unconscious to their own biases. This is closely related to gunnysacking.

Consulting Cap. A metaphorical cap, or hat, worn while offering consulting recommendations to a client. Typically, you might say, "I'm putting on my Consulting Cap now."

Cultural Expectations Around Respect. Some people and cultures have expectations around who is automatically deserving of respect (such as, the elderly, people in authority, etc.) This can create a disconnect in people's minds if the people they're required to respect are behaving disrespectfully.

Communication Styles. Each of us tends to unconsciously rely on a natural or preferred communication style. The DISC Communication Styles Assessment Instrument can help us identify our own styles and those of others. If we're unaware of how our style impacts others, we can inadvertently engage in behaviors that they consider disrespectful. The DISC assessment can help those coaching, facilitating, and/or engaged in the *CfR* process.

Deviant Workplace Behavior. Behavior in the workplace that crosses over a specific line into what is considered by experts in human resources and legal departments to be destructive, violent, dangerous, and illegal. The *CfR* process is not designed to address this kind of behavior.

Earned Respect. Some believe that employees must earn their manager's respect regardless of how the manager behaves. Typically, this backfires and results in the manager *not* being respected. They may be obeyed or feared, but they won't be respected. These days, this kind of work relationship in unlikely to be as productive as it once was.

Facilitator's Cap. A metaphorical cap, or hat, worn while facilitating the joint session with both participants together. The facilitator moves the phases of the joint session along and ensure both participants follow the process and the rules closely. Typically, you might say, "I'm putting on my facilitator's cap now."

Full Apology. A seven step process designed at the Center for Respectful Leadership that plays a pivotal role in *CfR*. Often a sincere *Full Apology* can be extraordinarily helpful in restoring respect to a broken relationship.

Gunnysacking. A process in which an employee will store perceived disrespectful behavior and microaggressions in a metaphorical sack which they carry around with them. Eventually, the sack can get too heavy, and they may make a formal complaint to HR, or engage in work slowdowns or other inappropriate behaviors, or quit.

It-Takes-Two-To-Tango. A concept in reference to the *CfR* process as a kind of "restorative dance" that both participants must willingly commit to and work on together during the coaching, the joint session, and afterwards. No work relationship can be repaired if only one person is committed to the process. One of the participants being out of integrity in the dance may be another reason you may have to shut the process down before it's completed.

Like vs. Respect. A core concept within Respectful Leadership™, it refers to research that indicates that you don't have to like someone to work productively with them, but you do have to have some level of respect for them, usually for their knowledge and experience, their talents and skills, and/or the way they treat you and others.

Mental Models. Unconscious beliefs and assumptions about others, relationships, and work processes, that may, or may not be helpful in establishing and maintaining healthy, respectful work relationships.

Neuroscience of Respect. Research that indicates that feelings of respect and disrespect are just that, "feelings," that result from very primitive threat responses in the brain and have little to do with cognitive, rational thought, at least when they first arise.

Restoring Respect

Out of Integrity. When a participant, or stakeholder, uses language or behaves in a way that you—as the Coach/Facilitator—consider insincere or manipulative. Or they go back on a commitment they've made or deny that they made the commitment in the first place. As coach, you're going to have to try to coach them back into integrity or determine if they are so far out of integrity that they cannot be coached back. In that case, you may have to shut the process down.

Performative Respect. Sometimes, when we don't genuinely respect someone, we engage in "performative respect" toward them as a way to "just get along." Occasionally the recipient of performative respect may perceive it as insincere and interpret as a "passive/aggressive" insult.

The Platinum Rule. Coined by Dr. Tony Allesandra, the Platinum Rule states, *"Do unto others as THEY would have you do unto THEM."* Unlike the *Golden Rule,* in which we assume *"it's good to treat others the way WE want to be treated,"* the *Platinum Rule* recommends that we *"treat others the way THEY want to be treated."* Leading according to the Platinum Rule is a core practice of Respectful Leaders.

Respect. Feeling and displaying genuine admiration and appreciation for someone based on their abilities, qualities, achievements, and/or position, or simply because they're another human being." Specific to "Interpersonal respect."

Respectful Leadership. A leadership style, developed by author Gregg Ward of the Center for Respectful Leadership, that places a premium on being respectful, empathetic, influencing, supportive, compassionate, kind, complimentary and civil to all stakeholders in an organization, including employees, managers, customers, vendors, the community, and the environment. RL is closely related to "Servant Leadership," and considered part of the practice of "Conscious Capitalism." You can learn about it in Gregg Ward's book *The Respectful Leader: Seven Ways to Influence Without Intimidation* (Wiley 2016, 2nd edition - Winding Creek Press 2018).

Request to Modify. Used in Step Nine, a "Request to Modify" is a request by either participant that the other modify their proposed behavioral change. You will facilitate the discussion around this request. But once it has been accepted or denied by the person who's being asked to modify their behavior, that's the end of it and the participants must move on.

Glossary of Terms

Restorative Dance. A metaphor for the *CfR* process in which both participants willingly work together to restore respect to the relationship. It's related to the It-Takes-Two-To-Tango concept.

Stakeholders. Others who are aware of the "what happened" and are either impacted directly, indirectly, and/or have a stake in the outcome (such as HR, Legal, and Leadership).

Sidebar. A private discussion with one of the two participants during Step Nine, the joint session. Typically, a Sidebar is necessary when someone is starting to waiver in their commitment to stay in the conversation, and/or is "out of integrity," and you need to coach them back to it.

Trust Gap. The distance between two people in terms of trust, measured by the closeness of their relationship. The larger the trust gap between them, the less trust they have and the harder it is to bridge that gap.

SMART Goals. An acronym used by managers to set goals: **S**pecific, **M**easurable, **A**ctionable (or **A**chievable), **R**elevant, and **T**ime-Bound.

Traditional Leadership Styles. Traditional leadership styles, such as "command-and-control," and "carrot-and-stick." While effective in some organizations (such as the military or sales), are no longer as effective as they once were. Also, they are considered disrespectful by many employees, again, especially millennials and Gen Z's. There is a newer, more effective leadership style, called Respectful Leadership™.

Toxic Work Environments. Defined as work environments in which employees aren't respected and/or which don't value diversity, equity, and inclusion and which tolerate unethical behavior. These are all key drivers of conflict, resignations, and poor performance, as well as a lack of collaboration and teamwork.

Unrightable Wrongs. Sometimes, people feel that the person who disrespected them has committed an egregious act of disrespect that they perceive it as an "unrightable wrong," and believe that nothing anyone says or does will change their mind about how they feel about that person. Unrightable wrongs are one of several reasons that may cause you to shut down the *CfR* process before it has been successfully completed.

Unintentional Disrespect. Most people, when accused of being disrespectful, will claim that that wasn't their intention. But intentions don't matter. If people feel disrespected, they feel disrespected. This will make it harder for them to work with the people who they believe disrespected them.

Verbalizing Emotions. Like psychotherapists use of "talk therapy," when you are coaching someone and you encourage them to specifically and repeatedly name the feelings they had when they felt disrespected, then eventually they can speak rationally about the "what happened" and their role in it without being triggered, or at least less so.

Wants & Needs. What each person in the *CfR* process needs from the other, and wants them to do, in order to move forward successfully with the work relationship.

The "What Happened." Events or incidents in which people used language and/or behaved in such a way that led to others feeling disrespected. It is important to note that someone can engage in disrespectful behavior toward others *and* feel disrespected by others' behavior at the same time.

Who Can I Control? Only Me. A concept referred to in the *CfR* process that underscores the fact that trying to control someone often backfires. A typical example is forcing someone to apologize. Participants being coached must understand that the only people they can control are themselves.

The Work World Has Changed. In the past, being respected at work was considered a nice-to-have. Today, the world of work has changed, and many employees have an expectation that they will be treated with respect. Whether we like it or not, this is our new work world. The most effective and respected leaders will adapt to these new paradigms.

You Don't Have to Like Someone to Work With Them, But You Do Have to Have Some Level of Respect for Them. At the Center for Respectful Leadership, we call this "the big idea," because it's one of the cornerstones of our philosophy.

Now that you've read *Restoring Respect*, get *The Restoring Respect Workbook*!

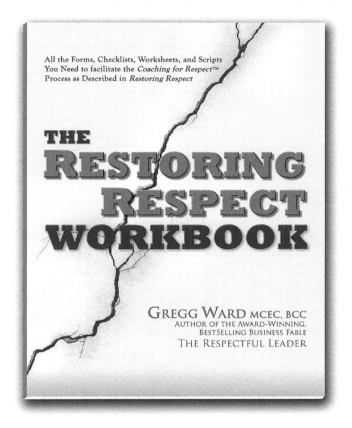

This inexpensive, easy-to-use workbook contains every checklist, fill-in form, and worksheet found in the original Restoring Respect book, all laid out on standard 8.5" x 11" sheets. ISBN 978-1-931957-22-9

- Photocopy or scan and print-out individual checklists, forms, & worksheets

- Buy one workbook for each "Restoring Respect/Coaching for Respect™ case that you facilitate.

**To order your copies of *The Restoring Respect Workbook*,
or to download PDF versions visit
RestoringRespectBook.com**

**To purchase bulk copies of *Restoring Respect* or *The Respectful Leader*
contact: hello@respectfulleadership.org**

Restoring Respect and *The Restoring Respect Workbook*
are both available as printable PDFs!

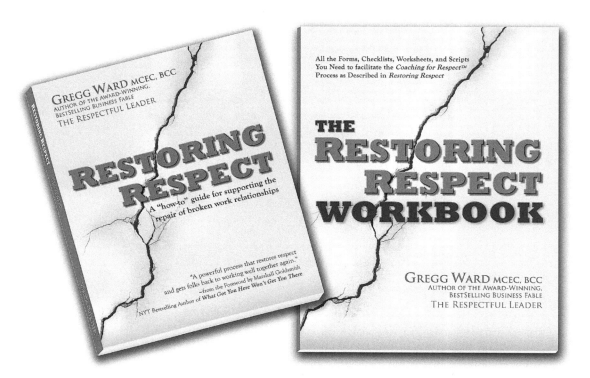

Restoring Respect PDF
ISBN 978-1-931957-21-2

The Restoring Respect Workbook PDF
ISBN 978-1-931957-23-6

Exclusively from
RestoringRespectBook.com

For more information about the Center for Respectful Leadership's work, training programs, executive coaching, and resources, visit:

CenterForRespectfulLeadership.org

To inquire about Coaching for Respect™ Certification program dates and locations, please email us at the Center for Respectful Leadership at:

Collective@RespectfulLeadership.org

About the Author

Gregg Ward is the Founder and Executive Director of the Center for Respectful Leadership and a bestselling, award-winning author, speaker, facilitator, and executive coach. He is on a mission to transform lives and organizations through respect and Respectful Leadership™. Gregg's second book, *The Respectful Leader* (John Wiley & Sons, 2016) was named a "Best Book of the Month" by Amazon and instantly became a best-seller in its category. In 2018, the book won the *Gold Medal* in the prestigious *Axiom Business Book Awards* competition.

Having trained and worked as a professional in theater, television and film in New York and the UK, Gregg began his career in learning and development as a specialist trainer for The NYPD using the techniques of live theater and improvisation to train police officers. Since then, Gregg has developed and delivered over 2,500 keynote presentations and talks, training programs, seminars, webinars, and workshops in North America, Europe, and the Middle East for groups ranging in size from 12 to 2,000.

Gregg's many clients include *ADP, AXA, Booz Allen Hamilton, Ericsson, Ford, Harley-Davidson, Intel, Kaiser Permanente, Premier Members Credit Union, Qualcomm, the US Navy, the US Department of Labor,* and *Warner Bros Studios.*

A prolific writer whose articles have appeared in *Forbes, Entrepreneur,* and *The San Diego Union Tribune*, Gregg also served for five years as a freelance journalist and feature writer on assignment throughout Europe for *Scotland on Sunday, The List Magazine, The Times of London,* and *BBC Radio-Scotland*. He is extremely proud to have covered the fall of the Berlin Wall.

Gregg holds a BFA from Boston University's College of Fine Arts, is a Board Certified Coach (BCC), a Master Corporate Executive Coach (MCEC), and an Executive Coach with The Center for Creative Leadership. He is certified in The Hogan, DISC, MBTI, FIRO-B, Workplace Big 5 and 360-Leader assessment instruments and received training in mediation from the National Conflict Resolution Center.

He lives with his partner Kathleen in San Diego and plays as much tennis as time and his body will allow.

Lightning Source UK Ltd.
Milton Keynes UK
UKHW050342150223
417031UK00024B/354